WHALES AND DOLPHINS
ATLANTIC CANADA & NORTHEAST UNITED STATES

TARA S. STEVENS

BOULDER PUBLICATIONS

Library and Archives Canada Cataloguing in Publication

Stevens, Tara
    Whales and Dolphins Field Guide: Atlantic Canada and Northeast United States / Tara Stevens.

Includes bibliographical references and index.
ISBN 978-1-927099-16-2

    1. Whales--North Atlantic Ocean--Identification. 2. Dolphins--North Atlantic Ocean--Identification. I. Title.

QL737.C4S74 2013   599.517'734   C2013-901435-7

Published by Boulder Publications
Portugal Cove-St. Philip's, Newfoundland and Labrador
www.boulderpublications.ca

© 2013 Tara S. Stevens

Editor: Stephanie Porter
Copy editor: Iona Bulgin
Design and layout: John Andrews
Main cover photo: Nadine and Thierry Vogenstahl
Back cover illustration: Trish Stevens

Printed in China

Excerpts from this publication may be reproduced under licence from Access Copyright, or with the express written permission of Boulder Publications Ltd., as permitted by law. All rights are otherwise reserved and no part of this publication may be reproduced, stored in a retrieval system, or transmitted in any form or by any means, electronic, mechanic, photocopying, scanning, recording, or otherwise, except as specifically authorized.

We acknowledge the financial support of the Government of Newfoundland and Labrador through the Department of Tourism, Culture and Recreation.

We acknowledge financial support for our publishing program by the Government of Canada and the Department of Canadian Heritage through the Canada Book Fund.

Dedication

To my wonderful parents, who urged me
to follow my dreams and passions.
This book is for you.

TABLE OF CONTENTS

Preface	7
Biological Oceanography	9
Methods of Whale and Dolphin Research	11
Killer Whales of the Northwest Atlantic: Research in Action	16
Threats and Conservation	20
How to Use This Book	23
Quick Whale and Dolphin ID	24
Baleen Species	30
Blue Whale	32
Fin Whale	36
Sei Whale	40
Humpback Whale	44
Bowhead Whale	50
North Atlantic Right Whale	54
Minke Whale	58
Toothed Species	62
Sperm Whale	64
Northern Bottlenose Whale	68
Cuvier's Beaked Whale	72
Long-Finned Pilot Whale	76
Killer Whale	82
Sowerby's Beaked Whale	88
True's Beaked Whale	92
Narwhal	94
Blainville's Beaked Whale	98
Beluga Whale	102
Risso's Dolphin	106
Common Bottlenose Dolphin	110
White-Beaked Dolphin	114
Atlantic White-Sided Dolphin	118
Short-Beaked Common Dolphin	122
Dwarf Sperm Whale	126
Pygmy Sperm Whale	126
Striped Dolphin	130
Harbour Porpoise	134
Glossary	138
Further Reading	142
Acknowledgements	143
About the Author	144
About the Illustrator	144

PREFACE

Whales and dolphins, also known as cetaceans, are found throughout the world's oceans. This field guide describes those 26 species found in the waters off Atlantic Canada and the New England states, from nearshore to far offshore regions. Many of these species are recognizable and well studied, others are poorly understood. The efforts of researchers around the world to get to know more about some of these elusive species are highlighted in this book.

From early traditional and subsistence whaling to modern commercial whaling, from legends and folklore to the "Save the Whales" movement, humans have always had a relationship with these important species. In the twenty-first century both researchers and the general public are showing more interest in learning about whale and dolphin biology, ecology, and behaviour. More complicated and contentious subjects such as how human activities directly and indirectly affect cetacean populations are also being studied. As a whale researcher, I can say this is an exciting time to be involved in whale and dolphin research.

If you live in or are visiting this part of the northwest Atlantic, I encourage you to take the opportunity to observe and learn about these great animals in their natural habitat. Let this book be your guide.

A humpback whale diving near Newfoundland and Labrador. *Tara S. Stevens / DFO*

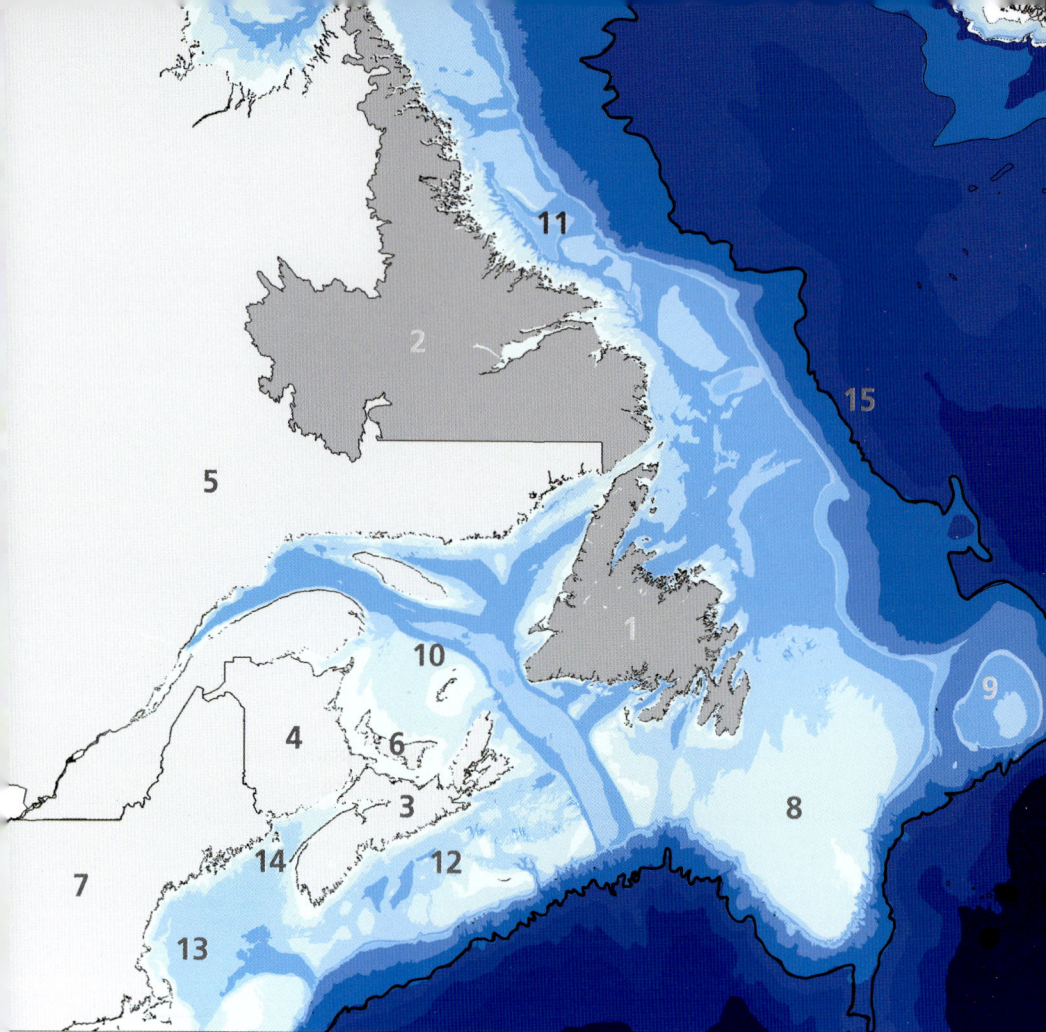

Map showing the bathymetry, or sea-floor topography, of the waters near Atlantic Canada. The lighter shades of blue indicate shallower water.

1. Newfoundland
2. Labrador
3. Nova Scotia
4. New Brunswick
5. Quebec
6. PEI
7. United States
8. Grand Banks
9. Flemish Cap
10. Gulf of St. Lawrence
11. Labrador Shelf
12. Scotian Shelf
13. Gulf of Maine
14. Bay of Fundy
15. Black bathymetry line: 3,000 m contour

BIOLOGICAL OCEANOGRAPHY

A dynamic region, the northwest Atlantic Ocean is characterized by high biological productivity. Understanding why the area is so rich in marine life also sheds light on why whales and dolphins inhabit this region in such abundance.

Four characteristics combine to make the waters off Atlantic Canada and the northeast United States one of the most biologically productive regions in the world: the shallow continental shelf, namely the Scotian Shelf, Grand Banks, and Labrador Shelf; the bathymetry, or underwater topography, of the shelf edge and banks; the Gulf Stream, a warm surface current flowing south to north and skirting the continental shelf edge; and the cold, nutrient-rich Labrador Current travelling south from the Arctic along the continental shelf.

At the base of the food chain is phytoplankton production, also known as primary productivity. Phytoplankton, microscopic photosynthesizing plant species that grow rapidly into "blooms" under ideal conditions, supply food to organisms in the water column, through direct or indirect consumption.

Based on species-specific chemical and physical thresholds, including light, temperature, and nutrients, an explosion of phytoplankton occurs in early spring and early autumn. These spring and fall blooms created by the abundance of photosynthesizing phytoplankton can be seen on satellite images as green discolourations of the ocean surface.

Zooplankton population levels rise and peak during and shortly after these phytoplankton blooms. Zooplankton are small, often microscopic, organisms in the kingdom Animalia. As with phytoplankton, their oceanic distribution is dependent upon ideal growth conditions. Zooplankton feed directly on phytoplankton and smaller zooplankton; this is the second stage of the food chain, or secondary productivity.

Zooplankton are consumed directly by some baleen species. For example, North Atlantic right whales feed exclusively on one species of copepod zooplankton, and blue whales feed on krill, another zooplankton species. Humpback and fin whales feed on small schooling fish—fish that prey on zooplankton. Although this oceanic food web is complex, all trophic levels on the food chain can be traced back to zooplankton and phytoplankton.

Intersecting waterways and continental shelf break

A lack of nutrients will limit phytoplankton growth. The interaction of hydrographic and physical features of the northwest Atlantic (listed above) support high levels of primary and secondary production growth.

The Labrador Current delivers cold, nutrient-rich waters to the shelf and banks regions of Atlantic Canada. These waters contrast with the warm northerly flowing Gulf Stream and literally create a physical barrier that microscopic planktonic organisms, phytoplankton and zooplankton, cannot cross due to extreme differences in the densities of the two opposing water masses. Additionally, northerly flowing bottom waters flow up toward the surface at the continental shelf break in a process called upwelling, which delivers nutrients to the surface. These mechanisms bring nutrient-laden waters to the surface in the northwest Atlantic and are critical to the region's biological productivity, both micro- and macroscopically.

Whales and dolphins are not distributed evenly across the northwest Atlantic. They live near the physical habitat and food they require. The biological and physical link between humpback whales and sand lance is an example. Sand lance, small schooling fish that feed on zooplankton, occur in areas where primary and secondary production provides high concentrations of their preferred prey. Humpback whales prey on small schooling fish, including sand lance. Not surprisingly, humpback whale distribution often correlates with that of the sand lance (and other prey species). As prey populations move and shift, cetacean distributions shift in response.

Researchers can deduce potential "hot spots," or highly productive areas, by considering seafloor and ocean characteristics. Bank edges and current fronts are typical locations of advantageous biological productivity. In the northwest Atlantic, these include the mouth of the Bay of Fundy, banks within the Gulf of St. Lawrence, and the shelf break from northern Labrador to the southern Grand Banks, Flemish Cap, and Scotian shelf. The combined effects of sea-floor bathymetry and hydrographic features facilitate vertical mixing such as upwelling, transporting nutrients that may be used by phytoplankton to initiate a web of productivity to the surface.

An ecosystem exploited

Contrary to the open ocean, which rarely receives an influx of nutrients from deeper layers of water, the northwest Atlantic is a dynamic, highly productive, and distinct body of water. The vertical mixing of ocean water maintains high primary productivity. This comes as no surprise to mariners, who have used this knowledge to obtain resources from the ocean.

Before commercial whaling and fishing, the northwest Atlantic—especially the Grand Banks and the Gulf of Maine—teemed with marine life. Fish were so plentiful in some regions that vessel movements were hindered. It was said that one only needed a basket to catch cod, and that the *Mayflower* was surrounded by whales upon its arrival at Cape Cod.

The Grand Banks in 2013 are not the rich fishing grounds they once were. Exploited fish species have been pushed beyond natural thresholds, and many have seriously declined or collapsed, including the Newfoundland northern cod. Other, less publicized species both above and below the cod's position in the food web have suffered similar ramifications. Taking fish from the ocean affects all levels of the food chain, including most whales and dolphins.

METHODS OF WHALE AND DOLPHIN RESEARCH

Whales and dolphins spend up to 95 per cent of the time underwater. Given this, the amount of cetacean research and the knowledge obtained about many species is remarkable. The ingenuity and dedication of cetologists have advanced our understanding of these animals—although, as becomes evident throughout this field guide, there is still much to discover.

Whale research began in the twentieth century during the modern whaling era. Regulations imposed by the International Whaling Commission ([IWC], created in 1946) stated that every whale killed and taken on board had to be examined and data collected from it. Whalers were required to take morphologic measurements such as length and girth, and examine stomach and, if female, uterine contents. Although some of the data may have been skewed from handling the dead animal (pulling a large, dead animal on board a whaling vessel usually resulted in a stretched-out whale, for example) or human error, the information collected provided baseline biological data for many species. Countries that are still whaling (Japan, Iceland, and Norway) must conduct examinations of the animals killed. For some species, this remains the greatest source of data. Much of the morphological data collected continues to be referenced as the best available estimates.

Cetacean research gained momentum as whaling declined in the mid-twentieth century. A strong movement toward using non-invasive research methods resulted. Although much can be learned from a dead whale, researchers sought to preserve their study species in the wake of destructive modern whaling. By the 1980s, most researchers collected information about whales and dolphins without killing them. Some of these non-invasive methods are outlined below.

Sighting and behavioural data

This is perhaps the most fundamental category of data collected on whales and dolphins. Sighting data such as date, time, location, and group size are collected and compiled into databases. Other important information includes the demographics of the group (the number of adult males, females, and/or calves present), the behaviour of the group or individuals (inter-group behaviour), and interactions or associations with other species at the time of the sighting.

All of this information can be collected with little, if any, interaction with the cetaceans. As expensive and technical equipment is not needed, nearly anyone can collect sighting information and submit it to researchers.

Photographic sampling

Photographic identification, or photo-ID, is another important and long-standing research technique. The goal is to photograph unique, obvious, and permanent identifying characteristics on individual whales, such as scars, nicks, and/or markings and colouration patterns. Documenting these features allows individual animals to be distinguished. Over the course of years and even decades, an individual animal can be tracked, provided it is seen and photographed.

Standardized sampling, such as restrictions to left-side dorsal fin photographs, is essential to creating photographic identification catalogues that can be used and shared by researchers. These photo-ID catalogues provide valuable information about individuals, groups, and populations. Photo-ID answers many questions about a specific population: abundance, movement and residency patterns, social organization, population demographics, and morphology characteristics.

Photographic sampling is generally conducted at close range (within 20 metres) from a small, maneuverable boat. For species that exhibit only slight variations between individuals, high-resolution images are needed to analyze slight pattern and marking variations. Long zoom lenses are required when photographing species for which close approaches are difficult. Encounters with some species are rare, and research trips to observe them are expensive. Researchers often invest in top-of-the-line cameras to ensure accurate photography.

Tissue sampling

Tissue samples from cetaceans at sea are gathered using a specially designed arrow with a modified tip to biopsy the animal. The arrow is typically shot from a crossbow or air rifle, although lances are also used. The arrow bolt and biopsy tip are designed to strike the whale, grab a sample of skin and blubber, bounce off, and then float in the water to be retrieved. The length of the stainless steel tip determines how deep into the blubber the sample will be; it is generally chosen depending on the target study species (skin and blubber thickness varies between species) and the research question being studied. A typical biopsy tip used by researchers in Newfoundland and Labrador for studies on humpback, fin, and killer whales, for example, is 2 centimetres in length and 0.8 centimetres in diameter.

Biopsy tissue collection allows for important and varied analyses. Genetic analysis determines local and worldwide genetic diversity within a species, relatedness among individuals in a population, and lineage profiles of some matriarchal-driven species or populations. Stable isotope and fatty acid analyses are useful for understanding the foraging ecology and sometimes the preferred prey of a species. Toxicology studies reveal contaminant loads and may be used to assess the risk posed by pollutants such as polychlorinated biphenyls (PCBs), dichloro-diphenyl-trichloroethane (DDTs), and other inorganic manmade chemicals.

When compared to similar studies of a particular species in a different area of the world, these studies have the capacity to expand the knowledge of a species as a whole.

Underwater acoustic sampling

Vocalizations, or the sounds emitted by a whale or dolphin, can consist of tonal sounds, whistles, and echolocation. Underwater acoustic monitoring records sound

Individual humpback whales are identified by the pattern on the underside of their flukes, which range from almost all black to almost all white. Each humpback fluke is unique, helping researchers track their movements and behaviour through photo-identification. The black fluke shows injury scars from a killer whale interaction. *Tara S. Stevens / DFO*

Getting ready to fire a biopsy arrow from a crossbow off St-Pierre-et-Miquelon. *Robert Basha*

A biopsy arrow hits a killer whale. *Jack Lawson / DFO*

in the frequency range of the vocalizations of the species of whale or dolphin being studied.

Most whales and dolphins are highly vocal, emitting and receiving sound as their primary method of information exchange. Given their dark, underwater habitat, sound is their most important sensory mechanism.

Frequency, the rate at which pressure in a sound wave cycles between high and low, is measured in cycles per second or Hertz (Hz). Frequency to the human ear is perceived as pitch, so an increase in frequency relates to a higher pitched sound. Humans hear sounds ranging from 20 Hz to 20,000 Hz (20 kHz), although actual sensitivity for most people falls in a narrower range.

A biopsy arrow striking a fin whale off St. John's, Newfoundland and Labrador. *Tara S. Stevens / DFO*

Cetacean vocalizations differ from species to species. Some sound behaviours, recorded during social interactions and foraging, are believed to be used for group cohesion and coordination. Some species' acoustic repertoires identify social or family groups. For example, it has been discovered that in some populations of killer and sperm whales, the acoustic repertoire of vocalizations can indicate genetic relatedness.

Researchers use both autonomous and attended acoustic sampling devices to record their target species' vocalizations, other cetacean and animal sounds, ambient ocean noise, and anthropogenic underwater sounds.

Satellite and radio tagging

Satellite and radio tagging offer researchers a wealth of information about an individual cetacean, group, and/or species. With advances in data technologies, satellite tags, in particular, have become smaller, lighter, cheaper, and more widely accessible and used. Marine satellite tags range from simple location-only transmitters to those that read temperature, depth, light level, and swim speed, and have advanced retrieval and data-storage features.

Tara Stevens (pictured) and Jack Lawson prepare to deploy autonomous underwater acoustic monitoring gear off the Burin Peninsula, Newfoundland and Labrador. *Jack Lawson / DFO*

Tags can be affixed to the back or dorsal fin of a cetacean by means of a lance, crossbow, or air rifle. A satellite tag is similar to a GPS unit—data collected is transmitted at user-defined intervals to orbiting satellites that then send the data to ground-based receivers and data-processing systems. The cetacean's location is pinpointed by triangulation, using at least two satellites within range of the tag. Data from the tag can only be transmitted to a satellite when the whale is at the surface as tags cannot communicate with satellites through the water.

For many types of location-enabled satellite tags, researchers can remotely access their data in real or close to real time, allowing them to track individual whales while the tag remains functional and affixed to the cetacean. The device does not need to be retrieved to access stored information since it is all relayed via satellite.

A killer whale approaches a boat of observers near St-Pierre-et-Miquelon. *Nadine and Thierry Vogenstahl*

KILLER WHALES OF THE NORTHWEST ATLANTIC: RESEARCH IN ACTION

The killer whale is the most widely distributed of all mammal species and occupies both nearshore and offshore areas of all the world's oceans, ranging from pole to pole and nearly everywhere in between. Not all populations are equally well studied, however: killer whales in the northeast Pacific have been closely studied since the 1960s, but those in the northwest Atlantic are comparatively unknown.

Few published reports describing killer whales in the northwest Atlantic exist. Prior to 2007, the last substantial data about these killer whales were published in a 1988 series of reports that evaluated what was known about their biology, behaviour, and status in the entire North Atlantic. For the western North Atlantic, researchers summarized literature and local knowledge for accounts of killer whales, including live sightings, strandings, and whaling records. Except for a few notes written about chance encounters with killer whales, scientific records describing this population were few and far between.

Individual killer whales can be recognized by unique marks, scars, and the size and shape of their dorsal fin and saddle patch. Based on research conducted off British Columbia during the late 1960s to mid-1970s, photographs of the whale's left side dorsal fin and saddle patch area became the standard for identifying individual killer whales.

While there have been some small-scale attempts to photograph and catalogue killer whales in the northwest Atlantic, the first dedicated and ongoing scientific research study began in 2006 by the Canadian Department of Fisheries and Oceans (DFO) in Newfoundland and Labrador. Preliminary results of minimum abundance, distribution, and group organization were published in 2007. Killer whale research in the northwest Atlantic has since studied population status, such as abundance and risk factors, social organization, acoustic behaviour, feeding preferences, range and movement patterns, and habitat choices.

The amount of information about killer whales in the northwest Atlantic in 2013 is significantly larger than the limited historical data amalgamated and published in 1988. The research is still in its early stages, however, and is only a glance into this population's ecology and behaviour.

Killer whales have been recorded in all regions of Eastern Canada, including the Gulf of St. Lawrence, Bay of Fundy, and Newfoundland and Labrador. The Committee on the Status of Endangered Wildlife in Canada (COSEWIC) identifies killer whales in Eastern and Arctic Canada as one population: the Northwest Atlantic/Eastern Arctic population. This particular Canadian population is recognized in 2013 as Data Deficient, which is a standard set by the Canadian Science Advisory Secretariat (CSAS) and refers to the fact that there is not enough data to determine population trends or assess risk levels.

The beginnings: Killer whale research in Newfoundland and Labrador

In order to assess the status of killer whales in the northwest Atlantic, more information on their abundance, distribution, and lifestyle was needed. In 2006, Canada's Species at Risk Act (SARA) funded a short-term study to be directed toward killer whales in Newfoundland and Labrador. With this support, DFO research scientist

The adult male killer whale has a tall, triangular dorsal fin; the juvenile's dorsal fin is shorter and curved. *Tara S. Stevens / DFO*

An adult female killer whale and her calf (visible below the water's surface).
Nadine and Thierry Vogenstahl

Dr. Jack Lawson and I conducted surveys in the Strait of Belle Isle area, where killer whales are observed on a semi-regular basis during the late summer months. We were prepared to photograph individuals and, depending on the encounter, biopsy and record the group(s) acoustically. During the two-week research trip, we encountered only a single group of killer whales, despite surveying the region by vessel for over 35 hours and travelling a cumulative distance of over 330 nautical miles. That trip did, however, generate many questions about the behaviour and ecology of killer whales in the area and prompt further ongoing analyses and studies.

Since 2006, Dr. Lawson and I have spent countless hours searching for killer whales from land, sea, and air. As a result, a network of individuals throughout Newfoundland and Labrador has been established who report sightings and gather photographs. We expanded the photographic and sightings data on killer whales in Atlantic Canada. Creating a photo-identification catalogue and sightings database was essential for further killer whale research. This project has since taken an expanded, multi-year approach to answering precise questions about this population's behaviour and ecology.

Research strategies: A varied approach

Prior to 2006, the general public and even many cetacean researchers knew little, if anything, of the existence of killer whales in the northwest Atlantic. The most knowledgeable were seasoned fishers, most of whom, when asked, would provide details about an encounter or two with the great "blackfish" or "killers" (two of many common names used by fishers in reference to killer whales) over their lifetime at sea.

This told us that our research had to begin from the ground up. Along with the typical poor sea and weather conditions in the northwest Atlantic, the scarcity of killer whales meant that even finding our study species would be a challenge. As a result, the best approach to understanding this population was a research strategy incorporating various techniques so that if one failed or became impossible, another might ensure that a rare encounter resulted in useful data.

Our research on killer whales in the northwest Atlantic relies heavily on photographic identification and sighting statistics. Other strategies include acoustic monitoring, biopsy sampling, and satellite tagging. As of 2013, research continues throughout Newfoundland and Labrador, the Gulf of St. Lawrence, Nova Scotia, the Bay of Fundy, and the Gulf of Maine.

Preliminary results: A basic understanding

A total of 836 sightings of killer whales have been recorded in the northwest Atlantic between 1758 and 2012, with most occurring in the last 10 years and commonly during the June-September period near Newfoundland and Labrador. Most sightings have been made close to shore; however, killer whales have been observed beyond coastal shelf areas and in water depths exceeding 3,000 metres. Fewer killer whale sightings have been recorded on the Scotian Shelf, in the Gulf of St. Lawrence, or in the northeastern United States, despite comprehensive aerial and vessel-based surveys in those regions. Based on the photographic records, a hundred, possibly several hundred, killer whales may inhabit the region.

The distribution, movement, and residency patterns of killer whales may be linked to those of their prey; they have been observed harassing, attacking, and eating marine mammals including minke whales, humpback whales, dolphins, and seals, and fish. Some killer whales appear to remain year-round in Newfoundland waters and have been sighted during the spring within pack ice, likely there to feed on breeding harp seals. A majority of reported foraging accounts have involved minke whales. Although there is no evidence of spatial or temporal migration, killer whales may be seen in certain areas during particular times of the year, suggesting that long-term site-fidelity patterns may exist within this population.

Synthesis: Only the beginning

The data collected on the northwest Atlantic killer whales are preliminary. Researchers are just beginning to understand the basics of this species' ecology, behaviour, and population status; research on these topics continues.

An adult male killer whale. *Nadine and Thierry Vogenstahl*

THREATS AND CONSERVATION

Although human-induced threats and risks to cetaceans have changed over time—from widespread commercial whaling to the effects of naval sonar, for example—they are ever-present. Some species show signs of a slow recovery since the whaling era; however, many are considered Endangered or Critically Endangered. Modern threats to cetaceans may simply be too new for the effect or trend to be realized. Without a doubt, cetaceans are susceptible to human activities and, in addition to continued research, warrant some level of protection or conservation from our activities.

Cetacean conservation ranges from the extreme actions of Greenpeace and Sea Shepherd activists to local government policies to international protection standards. Protecting whales and dolphins is not an easy measure. They are mobile and unbounded by political boundaries. A humpback whale found in the northwest Atlantic during the summer will pass through many political boundaries, all with different definitions of "cetacean conservation," during its migration south to the West Indies for the winter.

Some areas of the world, where cetacean research is high and public opinion favours protecting whales and dolphins, are putting significant resources into conservation. This includes disallowing harm, harassment, and hunting marine mammals and aims policy toward protecting their habitats. Prescribed shipping lanes and regulations about fishing, vessel speeds, noise disturbances, and ocean pollution are measures that can be enacted. Conservationists, researchers, and regulators seek a balance between policy, science, and industry to offer some species a protective advantage where possible.

While public opinion in North America has been strongly in favour of whale and dolphin conservation—and the enactment of conservation measures has followed—not all countries exhibit the same commitment. Contrary to basic conservation measures, many countries still allow some form of Aboriginal, subsistence, or even commercial whaling activities. Regulation is often at each country's discretion, and

MAJOR THREATS TO CETACEANS
(in no particular order)

- Direct human disturbance, including whaling
- Marine traffic, boating, and whale-watching
- Habitat degradation
- Acoustic disturbance, especially seismic and naval operations
- Marine pollution
- Interaction with fisheries
- Incidental capture and entanglement
- Competition with fisheries (for food)

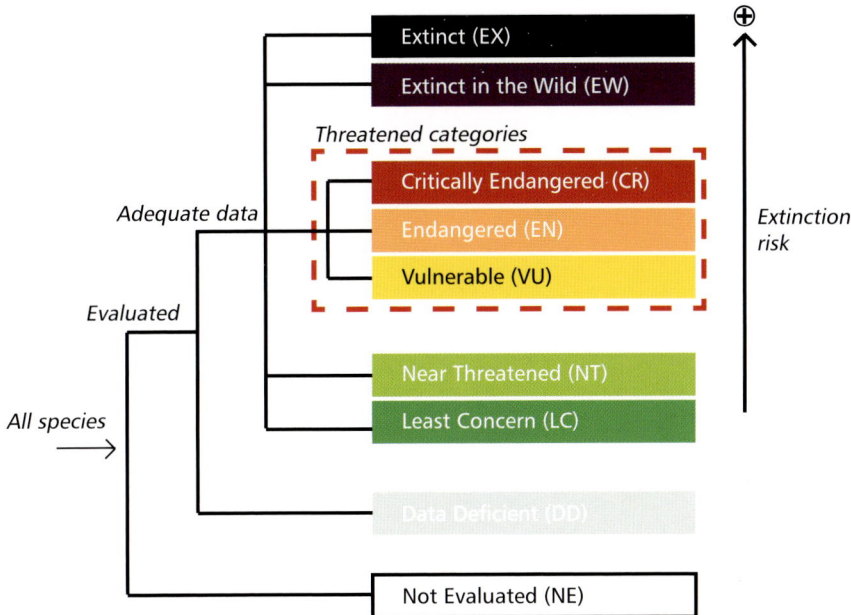

IUCN categories. Source: IUCN Red List

sometimes absent. Canada allows small hunts on bowhead whales by Inuit groups, which are regulated and managed by DFO. Most indigenous hunts are small scale, however, and do not threaten local whale and dolphin populations.

Threat levels (IUCN Red List)

The International Union for Conservation of Nature (IUCN) and its IUCN Red List of Threatened Species is globally recognized as the standard for evaluating the conservation status of plants and animals. This book uses the IUCN categories to indicate the status of each whale and dolphin species profiled. The chart on this page shows the increasing extinction risk, from Least Concern to Critically Endangered.

Due to a lack of data, many species cannot be properly evaluated; these are listed as Data Deficient.

Canada and US protection acts

Marine Mammal Protection Act (MMPA, US), 1972, amended 1994: Protection of all marine mammals (whales, dolphins, seals, manatees, polar bears), prohibits harassment in US waters and by US citizens on the high seas.

US Endangered Species Act, 1973: Identifies and protects all wild fauna and flora species in danger of extinction (Endangered) and those likely to become endangered (Threatened).

Species At Risk Act (Environment Canada), 2002: Offers protection for wildlife species at risk (expatriated, endangered, threatened) in Canada. This includes

A whale's blow is often the first thing whale watchers will see and can help with species identification. Some of the most distinctive whale blows are illustrated above: (top row, from left) North Atlantic right or bowhead (these are indistinguishable), minke, sei, blue; (bottom row, from left) fin, humpback, sperm, and killer whale. *Illustrations by Trish Stevens*

recommendations to avoid close approach distances and interactions/harassment with marine mammals.

History of whaling

- 3,000 BC: Earliest forms of shore-station and subsistence whaling began.
- 1,000 AD: The Basques started hunting whales through the North Atlantic.
- 16th century: The Basques set up the first whale-oil-production facility in the northwest Atlantic at Red Bay, Labrador. Right whales and sperm whales were targeted because of their relatively slow speed.
- 17th century: Early industrial whaling emerged, marking the beginning of the modern whaling era.
- 18th-19th centuries: Competitive, commercial national whaling began.
- 1860: The harpoon gun was invented; along with faster ships, this enabled whalers to chase and catch faster species, including blue and fin whales.
- First half of 20th century: Factory ships and large-scale whaling operations quickly decimate populations.
- 1930s: An estimated 30,000 whales were taken annually, marking the height of commercial whaling.
- 1946: IWC formed and established the first international hunting regulations.
- 1982: IWC voted for a worldwide moratorium on commercial whaling, effective in 1986.

HOW TO USE THIS FIELD GUIDE

The bulk of this field guide is divided into 26 chapters—one for each whale or dolphin species found around Atlantic Canada and the northeast United States (with the exception of dwarf and pygmy sperm whales; these rare creatures share one chapter). Each chapter is set up in the same way.

Whales and dolphins are classified as Baleen Species or Toothed Species

Illustration shows distinguishing features of the whale or dolphin

1-metre marker shows scale of painting

Key facts about the species, including information for quick identification

IUCN category, colour-coded according to the chart on page 21

Other interesting details about the species

Further information about each species' range, distinguishing characteristics, feeding and behaviour, population status, and threats

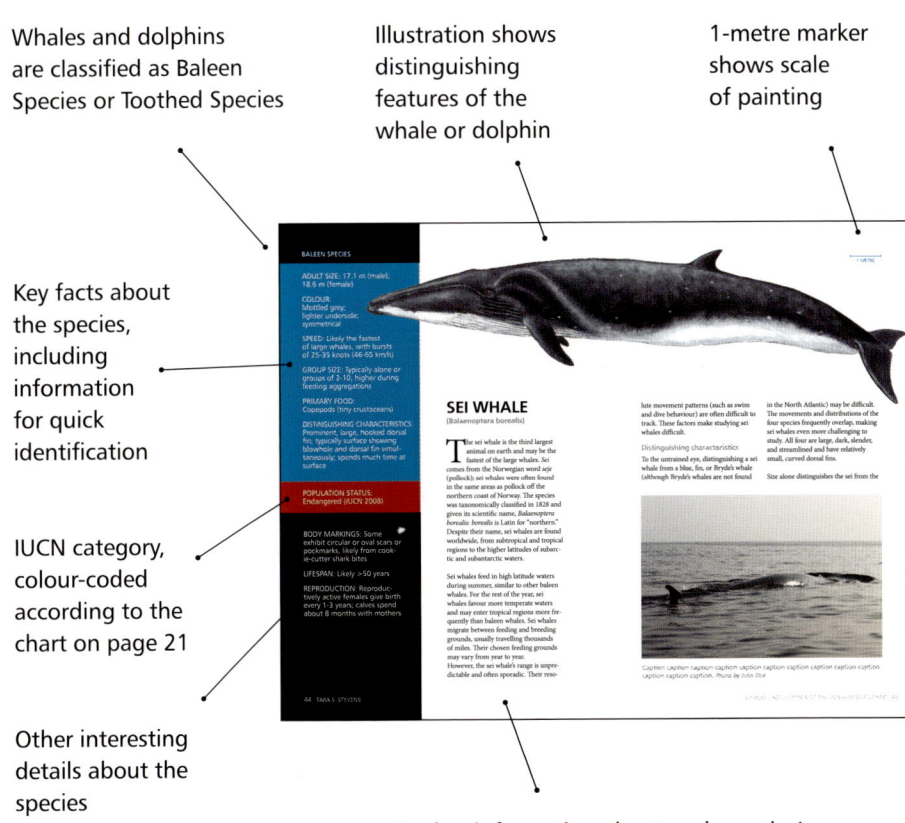

BALEEN SPECIES

⊢─┤
1 METRE
(Scale is approximate)

Humpback whale

Sei whale

Blue whale

24 WHALES AND DOLPHINS

TOOTHED SPECIES

1 METRE

(Scale is approximate)

Blainville's beaked whale

True's beaked whale (male)

Narwhal

Sowerby's beaked whale

Cuvier's beaked whale

Sperm whale

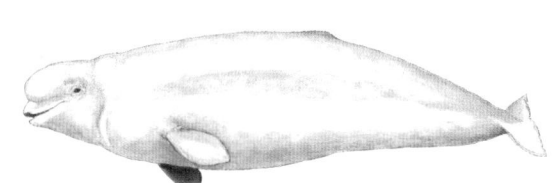

Beluga whale

Killer whale

Northern bottlenose whale

Long-finned pilot whale

ATLANTIC CANADA AND NORTHEAST UNITED STATES 27

TOOTHED SPECIES Continued

|———————| 1 METRE
(Scale is approximate)

Harbour porpoise

Pygmy sperm whale

Short-beaked dolphin

Risso's dolphin

28 WHALES AND DOLPHINS

Striped dolphin

Dwarf sperm whale

White-sided dolphin

White-beaked dolphin

Common bottlenose dolphin

ATLANTIC CANADA AND NORTHEAST UNITED STATES 29

BALEEN SPECIES

Mysticetes, or baleen whales, are a group of 14 species in the taxonomic suborder of Cetacea. They are characterized by the presence of slender plates of baleen inside their mouths, which serve as an elaborate filtration system for feeding.

Baleen, unique to mysticetes, enable these whales to efficiently feed on their main prey: small schooling fish and micro- and macroscopic zooplankton. Mysticetes engulf enormous quantities of water and prey; the ventral pleats on the lower jaw expand, increasing mouth volume. They then expel the water from their mouths by forcing it through the baleen, effectively trapping prey on the inside, which they then swallow.

A mysticete has several hundred baleen plates, composed of keratin (the substance found in human fingernails), hanging from the upper jaw along the outer perimeter on each side of the mouth. The inner surface of the baleen is composed of a fringe, which acts as the filter. Depending on the species, the fringe, or hair, may be very fine (predominantly among plankton-feeding species such as right whales in order to trap

The humpback whale's baleen is visible when its mouth is open.
Illustration by Trish Stevens

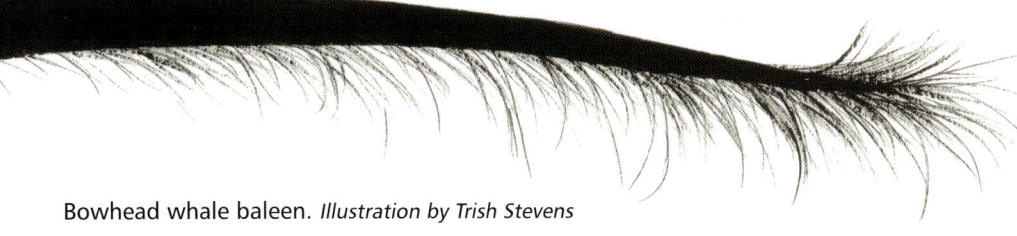

Bowhead whale baleen. *Illustration by Trish Stevens*

the tiny organisms), coarse (among species such as humpbacks that feed on larger prey including krill and small schooling fish), or somewhere in between (among opportunist feeders such as sei whales that take both plankton and fish).

Mysticetes are further subdivided into several families. Balaenopteridae, also known as rorquals, are the blue, fin, sei, Bryde's, minke, and humpback whales. With the exception of humpbacks, rorquals are sleek, streamlined whales suited for speed. They possess pleats, or throat grooves, that expand when the whale's mouth engulfs water. Bowhead and right whales belong to the family Balaenidae. These species are characterized by a robust, rotund body, no dorsal fin or ventral pleats, and long and narrow baleen plates. These whales are relatively slow and were an easy target for early and modern whalers, severely depleting most populations.

- Mysticetes are the largest of all whales (exception: sperm whales)
- Widely distributed, many species found in all ocean basins
- Some species migrate thousands of kilometres a year (humpback, blue, gray whales)
- Subject to exploitation from whaling, with most populations severely depleted, some to near extinction
- Four of the five "Great Whales" are mysticetes: blue, fin, Bryde's, and humpback whales (excluding sperm whales)

TAXONOMY

Kingdom: Animalia	Order: Cetacea
Phylum: Chordata	Suborder: Mysticeti
Class: Mammalia	4 families, 14 species

BALEEN SPECIES

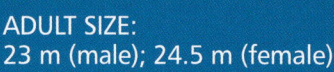

ADULT SIZE:
23 m (male); 24.5 m (female)

COLOUR: Mottled blue-grey; paler underside; uniformly blue head

SPEED: Bursts to 27 knots (50 km/h); typical travelling speed 10 knots (19 km/h)

GROUP SIZE: Solitary or in pairs, higher when feeding and breeding

PRIMARY FOOD: Krill

DISTINGUISHING CHARACTERISTICS: Large; blue-grey

POPULATION STATUS: Endangered (IUCN 2008)

GENERATION TIME: Approximately 31 years

ACOUSTICS: Vocalizations readily identifiable; often specific to individual populations or stocks

BREEDING: Nursing calves gain up to 4.5 kg/h; mother produces >200 L milk with 35-50% milk fat/day

BLUE WHALE
Balaenoptera musculus

The blue whale is the largest animal to inhabit the earth. Despite their massive size, blue whales feed on one of the smallest living creatures: krill. Although these whales are found worldwide, their global population has been severely depleted by commercial whaling. Between 70 and 90 per cent of the total population was taken in as few as three generations.

All subspecies of blue whales—North Atlantic and North Pacific (*B. m. musculus*), Southern hemisphere (*B. m. intermedia*), and Pygmy blue whales (*B. m. brevicauda*)—are classified as Endangered. Southern hemisphere blue whales, especially the subpopulations around Antarctica, are by far the largest of the three; North Atlantic blue whales lie midrange. Other subspecies have been suggested, such as Indian Ocean blue whales (*B. m. indica*), but little reliable evidence, such as genetic markers, exists for a formal reclassification.

Given their status, size, behaviour, and ecology, blue whales fascinate the public as well as scientists. Researchers are at a disadvantage, however, because blue whales are rare and tend to live offshore or in inhospitable waters.

Distinguishing characteristics

Despite their size, blue whales may be confused with other large mysticetes. Adult fin whales and, to a lesser extent, sei whales may rival the blue whale in size; all three have slender, streamlined, torpedo-shaped bodies.

Their blue-grey colour is solid on the head, mottled along the back and sides, and lighter along the bottom. Depending on the amount of light (sunlight versus foggy or cloudy conditions), blue whales can appear either more blue or more grey.

Blue whales have a large, broad, flat U-shaped head with a single distinctive ridge from rostrum to blowhole. The splashguard in front of the blowhole is noticeably larger than that of other mysticetes. The dorsal fin, small compared to its total size, is located approximately

A blue whale shows its fluke as it dives. *Nadine and Thierry Vogenstahl*

The single, prominent ridge from rostrum to blowhole is common to all blue whales. *Whitehead Lab, Dalhousie University*

three-quarters of the way back along the body. Finally, its blow is tall and slender and can reach 9 or more metres.

Differentiating the smaller pygmy blue whale from other blue whales is nearly impossible at sea, even by experienced observers.

Feeding and behaviour

Euphausiids, or krill, are the preferred and nearly exclusive prey of blue whales. These tiny shrimp-like marine crustaceans near the bottom of the food chain range from less than 1 centimetre to 14 centimetres in length—even the largest krill is only 1/218th the size of a blue whale. Krill are found in masses, allowing blue whales to engulf mouthfuls at once. Blue whales follow the krill's daily vertical movements to feed both at the surface and at depths of 100 metres. When they surface-feed, blue whales often lunge-feed, breaking through the mass of krill to come partially out of the water on their side or upside down.

Most, but not all, blue whales raise their flukes above the water when they dive. Short dives are most common, although they can stay under for up to 30 minutes. It is not uncommon for blue whales to breach, but the purpose of this behaviour is unknown.

Blue whales, most often alone or in pairs, are typically open-ocean animals. They congregate in larger groups closer to shore to feed and/or breed. Blue whales are distributed throughout Atlantic Canada but are most often observed in the Gulf of St. Lawrence during the summer feeding season.

As with other aspects of blue whale behaviour, migration patterns are poorly understood. Some blue whale populations are likely migratory, some resident. Migratory populations spend their summers in high-latitude, rich feeding grounds and then undertake long migrations to warmer tropical or subtropical waters to calve and possibly breed. Residents remain year-round in areas with plentiful prey.

Population status

The worldwide population of blue whales, considered Endangered by the International Union for Conservation of Nature (IUCN), likely meets the criterion for Critically Endangered. In particular, the once-massive Antarctic population was reduced by up to 97 per cent because of whaling.

A blue whale observed near Sable Island off Nova Scotia. *Whitehead Lab, Dalhousie University*

A blue whale surfaces near St-Pierre-et-Miquelon. *Nadine and Thierry Vogenstahl*

Approximately 400 individual blue whales have been photo-identified in the Gulf of St. Lawrence. There are an estimated 1,000 to 2,000 blue whales in the central North Atlantic. Still, sightings of blue whales, even off Norway and the British Isles, where they were abundant before commercial whaling, are rare in the North Atlantic.

The global population of blue whales is estimated to be in the 10,000-25,000 range. This means that the population is between 3 and 11 per cent of its early 1900s size. There is good news: the number of blue whales has increased since commercial whaling ceased.

Threats

Historically, the main threat to blue whale populations was direct exploitation through commercial whaling, which started in the North Atlantic in 1868. Blue whales have been protected worldwide since 1966, although illegal catches were made by the former Soviet Union until 1972.

Since blue whales are widely and remotely distributed, they may be at less risk than other whales to human impacts, including ship strikes and fishing-net entanglements.

Local populations, especially that of the Gulf of St. Lawrence, may be subject to disturbances and noise from vessel traffic. Other impacts, such as decreasing Arctic and Antarctic ice coverage and the possibility of inbreeding due to severely reduced population sizes, need to be better understood. However, there is no major known threat to the global population of blue whales.

BALEEN SPECIES

ADULT SIZE: 19 m (male); 20 m (female)

COLOUR: Dark to light grey; may appear brownish; white right jaw; dark grey left jaw

SPEED: Bursts to 25 knots (46.3 km/h); typical travelling speed 5-6 knots (9-11 km/h)

GROUP SIZE: Solitary or social groups of 2-7 individuals

PRIMARY FOOD: Small schooling fish (capelin, herring, etc.), euphausiids, and squid; schooling fish most common prey in north-west Atlantic

DISTINGUISHING CHARACTERISTICS: Large; asymmetrical lower jaw colouration (white on right side, dark on left); distinctive V-shaped head and pointed snout; curved dorsal fin; tall, narrow columnar blow, 9-12 m or higher

POPULATION STATUS: Endangered (IUCN 2008)

REPRODUCTION: Mature at 8 or 9 years

LIFESPAN: Up to 80 years

WHALING: Not targeted until late 1800s because of their speed and ability to evade early whalers

FIN WHALE
Balaenoptera physalus

The fin whale is the second largest animal on earth. This remains true even though the average length of fin whales has decreased significantly over the past 150 years—the longest specimens were targeted by whalers and thus removed from the gene pool. Records of fin whales measuring over 27 metres exist, but their maximum length is generally about 20 metres.

Fin whales in the northern hemisphere are typically up to 3 metres shorter than their southern hemisphere counterparts. As with all rorqual whales, male fin whales are shorter than female fin whales.

Fin whales are a cosmopolitan species, residing in all oceans of the world and into polar latitudes. Fin whales were heavily exploited by whalers, particularly since the early to mid-1900s. Some subpopulations have made great progress toward recovery, although pre-whaling population estimates far outnumber 2013 levels.

All fin whales have a unique asymmetrical lower jaw colouration: the left side

Fin whale, left side.

jaw is black, the right is white. The reason for this is unknown; one theory suggests that opposing colours are used when the whale is foraging to corral fish into tighter patches for more efficient feeding.

Distinguishing characteristics

Fin whales are distinguished by their size and colouration. Sleek, streamlined, and fast swimmers, they reach speeds over 16 knots (30 km/h), and their colouration ranges from dark grey to brownish grey with a white underside.

The front one-third of the baleen on the right side of the fin whale's mouth is white or cream. On sunny days, the white jaw is visible even if the whale is several metres below the surface. Occasionally, this can be mistaken for the white pectoral fin of a humpback whale, although identification is facilitated when the whale surfaces.

Leading from the head and upper jaw and along the back of the whale are light grey to cream-coloured swirl patterns,

A fin whale lunge-feeding, showing its white underside and expanding ventral pleats. *Nadine and Thierry Vogenstahl*

Fin whale, right side. Note the white lower jaw.

followed by a sideways V-shaped chevron that fades out along the back. The chevron, which is more pronounced on the right side than on the left, aids in identification.

Fin whale dorsal fins are often hooked; curve variation is an identifying feature. The pectoral fins and flukes are pointed, dark on the top and white underneath. Fin whales rarely show their flukes when diving.

Fin whales may be confused with blue, sei, and Bryde's whales worldwide. Bryde's whales, however, have not been observed in Atlantic Canada. Colour pattern, head and dorsal fin shape and position, and behavioural cues differentiate these whales.

Feeding and behaviour

The diet of fin whales is much less restricted than that of the larger blue whale. Fin whales feed on schooling fish, krill, or squid, and feeding varies from region to region, likely due to prey availability. Based on stomach content analysis, krill appears to be an important prey source for many subpopulations of fin whales, especially Icelandic and Antarctic stocks. Herring, capelin, and American sand lance are common prey in the northwest Atlantic. In many regions, the prevalence of capelin, for example, is highly variable, suggesting that fin whales are opportunistic feeders.

Fin whales are frequent lunge feeders, nearly always feeding on their right side. Other whale species favour one side over the other, although it has been suggested that fin whales' prey preference may be related to their asymmetrical colouration.

Fin whales usually travel or feed alone or in small, loosely associated groups of fewer than seven individuals. Large groups have been observed on some feeding grounds, but social affiliation among all members is unlikely. Segregation between sex and age class may occur in some regions.

Fin whales associate with blue whales, and interspecies mating, which results in a blue-fin hybrid offspring, has been proven. The occurrence and explanation for this may result from the small blue whale population size.

A fin whale surfaces in the waters between Newfoundland and St-Pierre-et-Miquelon. Note the distinct white jaw and emerging chevron pattern. *Nadine and Thierry Vogenstahl*

Fin whale migration is poorly understood. Reproducing adults do migrate but it is well documented that some remain on feeding grounds, including those in Atlantic Canada, during breeding season.

Population status

The IUCN lists the global fin whale population as Endangered. Since 1929, an estimated 70 per cent of the population has been destroyed by commercial whaling. The impact of such substantial catches remains unclear.

Some fin whale populations, such as those in the North Atlantic and Antarctic, may be recovering slowly, although it is unknown if these trends are long term and significant. The 2012 worldwide population estimate is around 53,000 whales, of which at least 3,000 are in waters off Atlantic Canada and the east coast of the United States. This estimate is a minimum figure; there are no comprehensive assessments for many regions within the expansive range of fin whales.

Threats

Fin whales are protected worldwide under many acts and management boards, such as the International Whaling Commission's (IWC) moratorium on whaling, the United States Endangered Species Act, the Convention on Trade in Endangered Species, the Convention on Migratory Species, and the Agreement for Conservation of Cetaceans in the Black and Mediterranean seas.

However, Norway, Russia, Iceland, Greenland (Denmark), and Japan hold provisions in objection to the IWC's moratorium and, as such, are not bound to treaties that restrict fin whale catch limits to zero. As a result, small Aboriginal subsistence hunts continue off Greenland and experimental and/or commercial

A close-up view of the fin whale's blowhole and white right jaw. *Nadine and Thierry Vogenstahl*

catches were resumed in 2005 and 2006 by Japan in the Antarctic and by Iceland in the central North Atlantic. Low catch levels of less than 200 per year worldwide are unlikely to have a significant effect on the global population. A return to high-effort whaling levels is not expected.

Of all large cetaceans, fin whales are the most common species reported in vessel collisions, and there are occasional reports of entanglement in fishing gear. These threats are unlikely to seriously affect the world population of fin whales.

On a positive note, fin whales may be better able to adapt to the effects of climate change than other large cetaceans. As fin whales are relatively opportunistic feeders, they may adapt better to changes in prey distribution, quality, and abundance.

Perhaps the most serious threat to fin whales is habitat degradation by acoustic disturbances. Fin whales produce low-frequency vocalizations for communication and other purposes. Increasing ocean noise is especially detrimental in low-frequency bandwidths. Masking, or covering up of the whales' vocalizations by anthropogenic noise, is an issue for many whale and dolphin species worldwide and may already affect fin whales.

BALEEN SPECIES

ADULT SIZE: 17.1 m (male); 18.6 m (female)

COLOUR: Mottled grey; lighter underside; symmetrical

SPEED: Likely the fastest of large whales, with bursts of 25-35 knots (46-65 km/h)

GROUP SIZE: Typically alone or groups of 2-10, higher during feeding aggregations

PRIMARY FOOD: Copepods (tiny crustaceans)

DISTINGUISHING CHARACTERISTICS: Prominent, large, hooked dorsal fin; typically surface showing blowhole and dorsal fin simultaneously; spends much time at surface

POPULATION STATUS: Endangered (IUCN 2008)

BODY MARKINGS: Some exhibit circular or oval scars or pockmarks, likely from cookie-cutter shark bites

LIFESPAN: Likely >50 years

REPRODUCTION: Reproductively active females give birth every 1-3 years; calves spend about 8 months with mothers

SEI WHALE
Balaenoptera borealis

The sei whale is the third largest animal on earth and may be the fastest of the large whales. *Sei* comes from the Norwegian word *seje* (pollock); sei whales were often found in the same areas as pollock off the northern coast of Norway. The species was taxonomically classified in 1828 and given its scientific name, *Balaenoptera borealis*: *borealis* is Latin for "northern." Despite their name, sei whales are found worldwide, from subtropical and tropical regions to the higher latitudes of subarctic and subantarctic waters.

Sei whales feed in high latitude waters during summer, similar to other mysticetes. For the rest of the year, sei whales favour more temperate waters and may enter tropical regions more frequently than other mysticetes. Sei whales migrate between feeding and breeding grounds, usually travelling thousands of miles. Their chosen feeding grounds may vary from year to year.

However, the sei whale's range is unpre-

1 METRE

dictable and often sporadic. Their resolute movement patterns (such as swim and dive behaviour) are often difficult to track. These factors make studying sei whales difficult.

Distinguishing characteristics

To the untrained eye, distinguishing a sei whale from a blue, fin, or Bryde's whale (although Bryde's whales are not found in the North Atlantic) may be difficult. The movements and distributions of the four species frequently overlap, making sei whales even more challenging to study. All four are large, dark, slender, and streamlined and have relatively small, curved dorsal fins.

The sei whale's relatively tall and hooked dorsal fin. *Nadine and Thierry Vogenstahl*

Observers watch a sei whale surface just before sunset. *Nadine and Thierry Vogenstahl*

Size alone distinguishes the sei from the blue whale. In the northern hemisphere, sei whales reach up to 17.1 metres (males) and 18.6 metres (females), while their southern counterparts are larger. The sei whale's taller and more hooked dorsal fin is located further forward on the body than on other mysticetes.

Sei whales are mottled grey with a paler underside; neither their flukes nor their flippers are white underneath. The fineness of their baleen as well as the relative shortness of their ventral grooves—although usually only observable on dead or stranded whales—also identify sei whales.

Feeding and behaviour

Sei whales are extremely fast swimmers and may reach burst speeds up to 35 knots (65 km/h), surpassing even the fin whale. Their extraordinary speed and erratic changes in direction allowed whalers to distinguish sei whales from other large mysticetes.

Sei whales are generally shallow skim feeders and will usually not dive very deep. When surfacing, they approach at a shallower angle than other rorquals and the head and dorsal fin often emerge simultaneously. Sei whales do not normally arch their tail stocks or raise their flukes above the water. Rather, they simply submerge beneath the surface.

Sei whales often feed on copepods and krill but may dive also for schooling fish and squid. They are opportunistic feeders; seasonal trends in diet have been documented. Nova Scotia's sei whale stocks prefer copepods and are not as diverse in their feeding.

Sei whales are often found in groups of two to five in the open ocean and at undersea shelf contours where upwelling brings nutrients to the surface and creates favourable feeding conditions. Sei whales are rarely found inshore or in coastal regions.

Population status

Relatively little is known about the life history of sei whales. Whaling in the early 1900s unquestionably had a negative effect on the species, although little was known of the population before it was exploited—and little is known now. This may be due to the sei whale's similarity to other large mysticetes, in addition to their preference for the open ocean, away from easily accessible coastal regions.

Surfacing sei whales often show both their blowhole and dorsal fin at the same time above the water's surface.
Nadine and Thierry Vogenstahl

An estimated 50,000 to 65,000 sei whales are left worldwide, although this figure may be distorted. Recent stock assessments of Canadian waters designated Atlantic populations Data Deficient.

Threats

Human-induced stresses, including ship strikes, entanglements, and, more importantly, habitat degradation by acoustic and chemical pollution, may be the most substantial threats to the sei whale's survival. They are better at evading humans than, for example, the fin whale, which makes research difficult but may help save their lives.

The sei whale's blow can reach 3-4 metres (10-13 feet) in height.
Nadine and Thierry Vogenstahl

Listed as Endangered on June 2, 1970, the sei whale is protected under the United States Endangered Species Act in addition to its status under the United States Marine Mammal Protection Act. The sei whales' most recent IUCN assessment listed the global population as Endangered in 2008, noting specifically that the most significant decline and lack of recovery took place in the Antarctic Ocean population; this is attributed to commercial whaling, which has ceased.

BALEEN SPECIES

ADULT SIZE: 15-16 m (male); 16-17 m (female)

COLOUR: Dark brown-grey to black topside, white underneath; white pectoral fins on both sides; fluke undersides have variable black and white patterning

SPEED: Average 2-8 knots (4-15 km/h), can reach 14 knots (26 km/h)

GROUP SIZE: Solitary or small, unstable groups of 10 or fewer individuals on feeding grounds; competitive groups of 20 or fewer males pursuing a single female common on breeding grounds

PRIMARY FOOD: Krill and schooling fish such as capelin, herring, mackerel, and sand lance

DISTINGUISHING CHARACTERISTICS: Knobby head, lower jaw, and pectoral fins; flippers up to one-third of body length; low, bushy blow; flukes usually raised when diving

POPULATION STATUS: Least Concern (IUCN 2008)

MIGRATION: One of the longest migrations of any mammal, can exceed 16,000 km round trip

ACOUSTICS: Male vocalizations in a "song," modified slightly year to year but consistent for all males

BEHAVIOUR: Among the most surface-active mysticete: full and half-breaching, lobtailing, flipper-slapping, and surface lunge-feeding; curious calves may approach boats

HUMPBACK WHALE
Megaptera novaeangliae

The humpback whale is likely the most recognizable and familiar mysticete, known for its spectacular aerial and surface displays—such as repetitive breaching, lobtailing, and flipper-slapping—as well as for its sounds and songs.

Individual humpback whales are identified by the pattern on the underside of their flukes. Their scientific name *Megaptera novaeangliae* translates as "giant-winged New Englander," referring to their long flippers and the area where they were originally identified as a distinct species. The humpback whale is the best-studied species of all the great whales: research began in the 1970s in the Gulf of Maine and continues worldwide.

A cosmopolitan species, humpback whales are found worldwide, from the

1 METRE

ice edge in the Arctic to that of the Antarctic, although they do not venture into ice fields as do other mysticetes such as the minke whale.

Humpbacks typically feed in high latitudes during the summer and then migrate to low, tropical latitudes during the winter for breeding and calving. Humpback whales undertake one of the longest migrations of any animal; some make a round trip of 16,000 kilometres.

Humpbacks are especially abundant in Atlantic Canadian waters during the summer. In the North Atlantic, six

A humpback whale spyhopping near researchers in the Bay of Fundy. *Kristin O'Brien / Whitehead Lab, Dalhousie University*

A humpback whale breaching. *Nadine and Thierry Vogenstahl*

Distinguishing characteristics

A humpback's body is large, stocky, and knobby, especially on its head, flippers, and tail stock. The round bumps on the head, called tubercles, are often encrusted with barnacles. Their pectoral fins are long, narrow, and bumpy along the leading edge. In the North Atlantic (as well as the southern hemisphere), humpback whale flippers are mostly white on both sides with a variable black border. Humpbacks in the North Pacific have white on the underside and black on the topside of their fins. In the North Atlantic, humpback whales have a white belly, which is variable in pattern and extent.

Body colour ranges from dark grey to blue-black to black and may show signs of scarring. The dorsal fin varies in size and shape. When humpback whales make a terminal dive, they raise their flukes above the water, showing an S-shaped, serrated trailing edge and individual black and white patterning

discrete feeding grounds are recognized: Gulf of Maine, Gulf of St. Lawrence, Newfoundland and Labrador, West Greenland, Iceland, and north Norway. Humpbacks show site fidelity, returning to the same feeding areas yearly, sometimes spanning decades. There are no subspecies of humpback whales, however, likely because whales from all feeding locations mix in common breeding grounds, such as the West Indies.

A humpback whale diving off Newfoundland and Labrador. *Tara S. Stevens / DFO*

Individual humpback whales are identified by the pattern on the underside of their flukes—each is unique, like a fingerprint. *Nadine and Thierry Vogenstahl*

on the underside. This pattern is akin to a fingerprint and ranges from all black to all white. The humpback whale's blow is low, round, and bushy and is greatly impacted by the wind.

Humpback whales are unlikely to be confused with other whale species at close range. Identification from a distance may be more challenging and, in the Atlantic Canada region, humpbacks are more likely to be confused with right, fin, and sei whales. However, fin and sei whales are larger and sleeker, glide faster through the water, and dive without raising their flukes. Right whales may be distinguished by the lack of a dorsal fin—the dorsal fin of a humpback is usually quite prominent.

Feeding and behaviour

Humpback whales feed on a variety of prey, including krill and small schooling fish. In the northwest Atlantic, humpbacks feed predominantly on fish, especially capelin off Newfoundland and Labrador and sand lance in the Gulf of Maine, but also on herring and mackerel. This is based on data from whaling records, which included records of the stomach contents of captured whales.

Like other mysticetes, humpback whales feed alone or in small, unstable groups in the North Atlantic. There is some evidence of long-term affiliations between individuals, but this appears to be uncommon. Cooperative feeding has been observed in some groups on North Atlantic feeding grounds. Bubble nets—circles of bubbles created by several humpbacks together underwater to corral fish between the ocean surface and the bubbles around them—is a unique cooperative feeding method. Humpbacks have been observed using their large, white pectoral fins to herd and trap schooling fish against shoreline underwater cliffs. The whales then lunge up through the confined group to engulf as many as possible. More commonly, though, humpbacks feed on the continental slope, where there are large concentrations of their prey. In the winter, when they are in their breeding grounds, humpbacks subsist on fat reserves gained during the feeding season.

Humpback whales are well known for the elaborate songs produced by males during the breeding season. In any particular ocean basin, all males sing the same song, making slight variations each year. Perceived by humans as calming, these sounds contrast sharply with the whales' breeding ground behaviour when they compete with other males to mate with a female. Males then are highly aggressive, displaying active tail slashes, lunges, charges, and blocks. Up to 20 males may vie for a single female.

Population status

Although humpback whales were heavily hunted during the commercial whaling period, their numbers worldwide have rebounded substantially. The species went from being on the IUCN Endangered list in 1986 to Least Concern in 2008. Worldwide, the estimated popula-

A humpback in the Bay of Fundy raises its pectoral fin. *Kristin O'Brien / Whitehead Lab, Dalhousie University*

tion is more than 60,000 and is increasing at an average rate of 3 per cent each year. In the North Atlantic, there were an estimated 11,570 whales in 2003. Factoring in the 3 per cent per year increase, this would put the total above 15,000 individuals in 2012 in the North Atlantic. This has not been substantiated.

Threats

Humpback whales worldwide have been protected from whaling since 1966. One or two whales have been taken annually since then in the form of "subsistence" whaling, mainly off St. Vincent in the West Indies.

In 2007, Japan announced it would defy the 50-year ban and take 50 humpback whales a year in the Antarctic for "scientific research," in addition to about 900 minke and 50 fin whales. Japan still has a quota of 50, although the hunt is not always carried out because of pressure from protestors. The effect of this hunt on local populations is unclear; however, these small-scale directed kills are not likely to jeopardize the species' recovery.

The greatest threats to humpback whales are entanglement in fishing gear and injury or death by ship strikes. Offshore oil and gas developments throughout the humpback's range can negatively impact the acoustic environment in which they live and vocalize. Although humpback whales do not sing while they are in their feeding grounds, they do occasionally vocalize; the effects of increasing anthropogenic noise are likely negative and warrant continued research and conservation action.

A humpback whale in the waters off St-Pierre-et-Miquelon lobtailing, or slapping the water, with its fluke.
Nadine and Thierry Vogenstahl

BALEEN SPECIES

ADULT SIZE: 15 m, both sexes

COLOUR: Black; white chin and, occasionally, white patch on tail stock

SPEED: Swimming speeds ~1-2 knots (2-4 km/h)

GROUP SIZE: Solitary or groups of 3-4; social bonds weak to non-existent, except mother-calf pairs; up to 50 in feeding aggregations or when confined by sea ice

PRIMARY FOOD: Krill and copepods

DISTINGUISHING CHARACTERISTICS: Large, robust head up to one-third body length; black and white colouration; rotund body; no dorsal fin; V-shaped blow; often fluke-up for terminal dive

POPULATION STATUS: Least Concern (IUCN 2008)

ACOUSTICS: Highly vocal; called "noisy" by Arctic researchers; low-frequency sounds (30-50 Hz) most common vocalizations; males' songs (up to 5 kHz) are comparable to humpback whale breeding songs

LIFESPAN: Over 100 years; possibly longest-living mammal

BOWHEAD WHALE
Balaena mysticetus

The Latin name for the bowhead whale translates to "whale" (from the Latin *balaena* and *cetus*) and "moustached" (from the Greek *mustakos*). The moustache refers to the bowhead's long baleen: adults can have up to 360 baleen plates, some of which exceed 4 metres in length.

Bowhead whales inhabit only the Arctic and subarctic regions in the northern hemisphere. They are highly adapted to survive in cold waters, preferring to live near pack ice: they follow the receding ice edge to the high Arctic during the summer, moving to lower latitudes during the winter as the ice advances south. To withstand this cold, bowhead whales have a 50-centimetre-thick blubber layer and a large head that breaks breathing holes in ice up to 1.8 metres thick.

The bowhead whale's circumpolar range is classified into five distinct subpopulations by the IWC: the largest, the Bering-Chukchi-Beaufort seas stock; and the nearest to Atlantic Canada, the Hudson Bay-Foxe Basin and Davis Strait-Baffin Bay stocks. While bowheads are not a common species in the northwest Atlantic (excluding Arctic Canada), their range extends down the Labrador coast. The extent of their southern movements relates to a particular year's sea-ice coverage, which is becoming more variable.

Bowhead whales are occasional visitors to Newfoundland. Usually lone juveniles displaced from their mothers, they are commonly stranded in remote areas around the island of Newfoundland and the south coast of Labrador. This trend has not been adequately researched.

Distinguishing characteristics

Bowhead whales, a large, robust, and rotund species, are relatively easy to identify at sea. The name "bowhead" comes from its bow-shaped jawline, fitting a head that is nearly one-third its body length. Its body is black, except for an irregular white chin containing a

A bowhead whale spyhopping in Isabella Bay, Baffin Island. *Pierre Richard*

line of black spots and, on some adults, a light grey band around the narrowest portion of its tail stock.

Bowhead whales have a prominent ridge in front of the blowhole and a deeper depression behind it. They do not have dorsal fins. They have broad, triangular flippers and large flukes with a middle notch that rises above the water on a terminal dive. Their blow appears V-shaped if seen from the front or back.

The bowhead's black and narrow baleen plates are the longest of any cetacean and measure up to 4.3 metres. Bowhead whales are similar in appearance to North Atlantic and North Pacific right whales, but a lack of light-coloured callosities (raised, bumpy patches of skin found on right whales) and the white chin of the bowhead facilitate identification. Their distributions rarely overlap, as right whales do not generally associate with sea ice.

Feeding and behaviour

Bowhead whales feed mainly on small to medium-sized crustaceans, with a preference for krill and copepods. They concentrate in areas where oceanographic processes create highly productive regions of prey aggregates. Bowheads also feed on mysids and amphipods (both small shrimp-like crustaceans) and some 60 other species. Like right whales, bowheads whales are skim feeders: they skim a path at the ocean's surface with their mouths open to collect and strain prey. They also feed at depth and near the ocean bottom.

Bowhead whales are usually solitary feeders, although occasionally small groups form to feed in echelon formation. For example, a concentration of zooplankton could attract several bowheads to the same area; even though the whales lack social bonds, they may occasionally align and coordinate their efforts to maximize foraging efficiency. Low frequency vocalizations between individuals may be used in these situations.

Acoustics affect bowhead whale behaviour. Although social bonds are weak to non-existent, except between mother-calf pairs, vocalizations are common and can travel long distances. The type of vocalization is often contingent on season and activity. During spring mating season, male bowheads produce songs analogous to well-known humpback songs to announce their fertility to females and to compete with other males. Bowheads likely also use vocalizations as a rudimentary form of echolocation, possibly to detect obstructions such as icebergs while they are travelling.

Since bowhead whales live primarily in Arctic and subarctic latitudes, research is nearly impossible during late fall and winter due to darkness and adverse ice and sea conditions. New research tools, such as autonomous acoustic monitoring and satellite tags, however, enable scientists to learn more about bowhead whale behaviour during those parts of the year when it was impossible to do so.

Population status

Bowhead whales were extensively targeted during the early whaling era, beginning in the 1500s. As a result, all subpopulations of bowhead whales were severely depleted. Northwest Atlantic populations were among the first to be exploited, with Basque whalers hunting extensively from Labrador to Spitsbergen, Svalbard (Norway).

Unlike the population of similarly exploited North Atlantic right whales, the

A bowhead whale surfaces in the Arctic Ocean, near the Northwest Territories. Note the long strands of algae wrapped around its snout.
John K.B. Ford / SeaPics.com

bowhead whale global population has shown signs of recovery. The worldwide population trend is officially classified as Increasing. The bowhead whale was considered Endangered in 1986; as of 2013, the species is listed as Least Concern by the IUCN. Some subpopulations remain severely depleted and, if considered separately, would be listed as Endangered. It is estimated that there are over 21,000 bowhead whales.

Although stocks are still far below pre-whaling population estimates, some have shown significant increases. The Bering-Chukchi-Beaufort subpopulation, for example, monitored from the 1970s to 2013, has increased 3.4 per cent per year. For a long-lived, large whale with a generation time of approximately 52 years, this recovery is notable.

Traditional Inuit knowledge and recent increases in bowhead sightings in Canadian Arctic and West Greenland waters may indicate that the population in these areas is also recovering. It is impossible to prove this scientifically; more sightings could also represent a changing or expanding geographic distribution, a theory which has been corroborated with quantitative data.

Threats

Aboriginal and subsistence whaling on some bowhead whale stocks is permitted by the IWC. The number of takes is small and Aboriginal hunts in Canadian waters by Alaskans and the Russian Federation is strictly monitored. These hunts have not interfered with the bowhead's recovery, although pressure on the Canadian government, in particular, to increase the allowed takes in the northwest Atlantic may threaten local populations.

Perhaps the most serious threats to bowhead whales worldwide are acoustic disturbance from oil and gas exploration and naval activities and the projected reduction of Arctic sea ice due to climate change. Because sound affects the behaviour and biology of bowhead whales, increasing anthropogenic ocean noise may be detrimental to this species. Because its habitat preference, feeding patterns, and seasonal migrations are linked to the extent and movement of pack ice, an extreme reduction or complete loss of Arctic sea ice may negatively impact this species. Close monitoring of this relationship is important.

BALEEN SPECIES

ADULT SIZE: 13-16 m; males usually 1-1.5 m shorter than females

COLOUR: Entirely black with variable white patches on belly; head callosities white to grey to yellowish brown, variable among individuals

SPEED: Slow swimmers, average 3 knots (6 km/h), maximum 5 knots (9 km/h)

GROUP SIZE: Solitary or loosely associated groups; feeding aggregations up to 150 whales; courtship or breeding groups up to 30 whales

PRIMARY FOOD: Copepods

DISTINGUISHING CHARACTERISTICS: Large, rotund, broad body shape; no dorsal fin; head callosities; V-shaped blow; flukes usually raised for terminal dive

POPULATION STATUS: Endangered (IUCN 2008)

LIFESPAN: Exceeds 70 years

POPULATION: Fewer than 350 in 2011

BREEDING: Reproductively active females deliver one calf every 3-5 years under optimal conditions; gestation about 12 months

NORTH ATLANTIC RIGHT WHALE
Eubalaena glacialis

The North Atlantic right whale was once abundant across the North Atlantic. There may have been tens to hundreds of thousands in the western North Atlantic. But the right whale was an easy and high-quality target for whalers, and the population was drastically reduced. As of 2011, North Atlantic right whales number fewer than 350. The species is being studied in order to preserve it.

The western North Atlantic population of right whales is considered highly Endangered; the eastern population is either Critically Endangered or possibly Extinct. Only eight right whale sightings were reported in the eastern North Atlantic from 1960 to 1999, one of which was identified as being from the western North Atlantic stock.

1 METRE

Based on DNA research, in 2000 the worldwide population of right whales was reclassified into three separate species: the North Atlantic right whale (*Eubalaena glacialis*), North Pacific right whale (*E. japonica*), and, in the southern hemisphere, the southern right whale (*E. australis*). Not all marine mammal scientists agree that they are separate species—often it depends on a scientist's definition of "species."

Distinguishing characteristics

The North Atlantic right whale is identified by its robust, rotund body shape, lack of dorsal fin, and callosities on its head and face. Callosities are rough, thick patches of skin, comparable to a callus, which occur only on hair follicles. Right whale callosities, caused by an infestation of cyamids (whale lice), are white to cream coloured. Individual right whales are identified by their pattern of callos-

A North Atlantic right whale diving in the Bay of Fundy near New Brunswick.
John G.T. Anderson

ATLANTIC CANADA AND NORTHEAST UNITED STATES 55

ities, which differs in size, shape, and placement.

Right whales are, overall, nearly entirely dark grey or black, except for a white patch on the belly behind the pectoral fins. Their flippers and fluke are broad and triangular; when the right whale dives, it usually raises its fluke above the water's surface. Right whales have an upward arched mouthline and, if viewed from above, a narrow rostrum. Their two blowholes are separated, creating a V-shaped blow.

The only other whale in the northwest Atlantic that may be confused with the North Atlantic right whale is the bowhead, but a lack of callosities and the bowhead's white chin set them apart. As well, the geographic range of bowhead whales and right whales rarely overlap.

Feeding and behaviour

North Atlantic right whales feed exclusively on plankton and zooplankton. Their prey of choice: copepods, specifically *Calanus finmarchicus*. Right whales are primarily surface skim feeders, slowly swimming along at the surface with their mouths open and filtering small prey through their fine baleen. Gatherings, sometimes of 150 whales, may form around a good feeding area, but right whales typically feed alone with no signs of collaboration while foraging amid other whales.

During the breeding season, courtship groups of up to 30 individuals may form. Males actively compete to get close and court a female. This surface-active group roll, splash, and churn the water for the right to mate. Although right whales are slow and awkward swimmers, they are surprisingly energetic when they congregate. They frequently breach, half-breach, lobtail, flipper-slap, and approach boats with curiosity. They are vocal, especially at night, on feeding grounds. Researchers are focusing on detecting right whales by acoustics as well as understanding the significance of their vocalizations.

Like other mysticetes, North Atlantic right whales exhibit seasonal migration patterns that, for most individuals of the population, are well known and consistent over many years. Although their primary feeding grounds are in the Gulf of Maine, Bay of Fundy, and Scotian Shelf, some individuals have been observed in the eastern Gulf of St. Lawrence and, rarely, Newfoundland, Iceland, and Norway. During fall and winter, they migrate south along the eastern United States seaboard to their calving grounds off Florida and Georgia. Courtship-type behaviour is observed year-round, although calving occurs only in the winter after a 12-month gestation.

Population status

The North Atlantic right whale is considered Endangered throughout its range. However, the eastern North Atlantic subpopulation is actually Critically Endangered, Possibly Extinct. Following heavy whaling from 1530 to 1935, when the IWC banned hunting of this species, the population remains at a critical level. As of 2013, the population trend is unknown, but its numbers fluctuate yearly between 250 and 300.

In 1998, it was estimated there were only 70 reproductively active female North Atlantic right whales. Fluctuating environmental conditions, high mortality rates, fluctuating calf survival rates, poor nutrition, and the poor health of the whales have led to variable calf production and calving intervals. In 1996, reproductively active females gave birth,

A North Atlantic right whale surfaces in the Bay of Fundy, near New Brunswick. Note the callosities on its head. *John G.T. Anderson*

on average, every 3.2 years; in the late 1990s, this figure was as high as 5.7 years. The low reproductive rate, coupled with a high mortality rate associated with human activities, hampers the possibility of recovery.

Threats

The most significant threats for the North Atlantic right whale are entanglement in fishing gear and mortality due to ship strikes. An estimated 10-30 per cent of the North Atlantic right whale population becomes entangled in fishing gear each year, with an average mortality rate of 1.6 individuals. Approximately one right whale dies each year because of collision with a vessel. Because of the small total population, these numbers have a significant impact on the species.

United States and Canadian regulations are attempting to reduce the number of right whale mortalities. In areas of eastern United States water where right whales are common, certain modifications and restrictions on fishing gear are required by law. The Mandatory Ship Reporting Scheme was enacted in 1999 in two important areas of calving and summering grounds. This system notifies vessels moving through or toward a particular area of the presence of right whales. Minimum approach distances and maximum speeds are enforced.

The International Maritime Organization approved an appeal to move some shipping lanes and to impose maximum transit speeds in the Bay of Fundy to avoid areas of right whale concentration in particular summering areas. Scientists and activists continue to petition for more regulatory actions from the United States and Canadian governments to further preserve this species.

BALEEN SPECIES

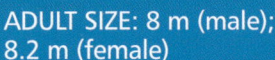

ADULT SIZE: 8 m (male); 8.2 m (female)

COLOUR: Dark grey to black body; white underside; paler side streaks

SPEED: Bursts to 24 knots (44 km/h); typical travelling speed ~12 knots (22 km/h)

GROUP SIZE: Typically alone, rarely in pairs; sometimes aggregate at feeding areas

PRIMARY FOOD: Small schooling fish, krill, and even marine crustaceans

DISTINGUISHING CHARACTERISTICS: Relatively small, torpedo-shaped body; light-coloured side streaks may extend to head; wide horizontal white band in centre of each pectoral fin; large, hooked dorsal fin

POPULATION STATUS: Least Concern (IUCN 2008)

DISTRIBUTION: Can occur in pack ice near the poles (may be an avoidance measure from natural prey such as killer whales)

MINKE WHALE
Balaenoptera acutorostrata

The minke whale, the smallest and most abundant of mysticetes, has two separately identified species: the common minke whale (*Balaenoptera acutorostrata*) and the Antarctic minke whale (*B. bonaerensis*), which exists only in the Antarctic Ocean. Minke whales in the North Atlantic, including the Canadian and United States east coast stock, are *B. acutorostrata*, referred to as the minke whale.

A cosmopolitan species, the minke whale is found in all oceans and nearly all latitudes north and south of the equator. It is common in the northern North Atlantic, including nearshore and offshore Atlantic Canada, during the summer. It is clear that at least some individuals of the North Atlantic minke whale population overwinter in the higher-latitude summer range.

Minke whales were exploited during

commercial whaling, especially since the 1940s after the population of larger, more valuable whales had been drastically diminished. The largest catches of minke whales were made in the northeast Atlantic by Norwegian whalers, who took approximately 120,000 of the 140,000 recorded catches in the entire North Atlantic. From 1948 to 1972, there was a small-scale fishery for these whales in Newfoundland; worldwide catches were phased out by 1987. Since 1993, however, some countries have resumed commercial whaling for minke whales, although at a much lower level.

Distinguishing characteristics

Minke whales exhibit the streamlined body design of other mysticetes, but with a more pointed head, making them torpedo shaped and typically easy to identify at sea and from the air.

Minke whales are dark grey to black with a white belly and lighter lateral streaks or bands that may extend to the head. Perhaps the most useful characteristic for identification is the single wide white band across the centre of each pectoral fin. This band is visible when the whale is completely submerged near the surface of the water, especially on sunny days. The absence of a visible blow is also characteristic; if a blow is seen, it is usually diffuse and small. The dorsal fin is large, hooked, and positioned about two-thirds of the way back from the rostrum.

A minke whale's distinct pointed head allows easy identification. *Nadine and Thierry Vogenstahl*

A minke whale surfaces near St-Pierre-et-Miquelon. The white band across its pectoral fin is visible through the water. *Nadine and Thierry Vogenstahl*

Minke whales are probably the easiest rorqual to identify on the basis of their size, colouration, dorsal fin shape, and lack of a blow. Other whales that may be confused with minke whales, usually from a distance, are sei, Bryde's, and some beaked whales.

Feeding and behaviour

Minke whales have a diverse range of prey species and types, which is unusual among whales. Their main food sources are krill and small schooling fish such as herring and capelin. Other prey, including bony fish such as cod and even crustaceans, have been found in their stomachs. The diet of minke whales in the North Atlantic varies by area and year, depending on prey availability.

Common in both coastal and offshore waters, minke whales are found alone or, less often, in pairs. They may gather while feeding but do not usually cooperate. Although dozens may be spread over a wide area, this does not, however, denote any association as group members. Minke whales do not show their flukes while diving but can be seen breaching, sometimes in sequences up to 10 or more breaches.

Population status

Minke whales are ranked Least Concern by the IUCN and the population trend listed as Stable. As a species targeted by some whaling nations, this population classification and trend is encouraging. In the North Atlantic alone, which includes four separately estimated stocks

(Northeast Atlantic, Central North Atlantic, West Greenland, and Canadian and United States East Coast), the best population estimate is about 182,000 minke whales. This is likely an underestimate, as an estimate for the Newfoundland and Labrador area, which has a substantial population of minke whales, is not yet available.

A reliable method by which to determine the age of individuals has not been found. The estimated generation time for this species is 22 years, but this could be drastically skewed.

Threats

Although minke whaling was phased out by 1987, it resumed—at a lower rate—in 1993 and is still carried out by Norway, Greenland (Denmark), and Iceland. Hunting continues to be a threat, although the number of takes per year (less than 2,000 as of 2013) is unlikely to threaten the survival of North Atlantic minke whales.

The low and diffuse blow of a minke whale is rarely seen. *Nadine and Thierry Vogenstahl*

Incidental catches in fishing gear occur throughout the North Atlantic range of minke whales, although this too is unlikely to negatively affect the population. Decreasing coverage of polar sea ice could present problems to this population, either directly or through secondary or tertiary effects, although it is unclear whether these would be positive or negative.

Like most whales, minke whales use sound to communicate, possibly navigate, and otherwise live in an underwater environment where visual cues are minimal. As sea traffic, fishing, naval experiments, and oil exploration increase, the undersea acoustic environment becomes increasingly noisy. This could lead to the displacement of minke whales, changes in behaviour, or even deafness and death. These effects must be monitored.

Unlike most other rorquals, minke whales are prey for certain types of killer whales. This is especially true around Newfoundland and Labrador, where sightings of minke whale kills by killer whales are prevalent. Given the small population of killer whales relative to that of minke whales, it is unlikely that this threat will influence the overall population of minke whales in the North Atlantic.

A hooked, relatively large dorsal fin is a distinguishing characteristic of this species. *Nadine and Thierry Vogenstahl*

TOOTHED SPECIES

Odontocetes, or toothed species, are whales and dolphins that have teeth as opposed to baleen (mysticetes). This is a large suborder within the order Cetacea, containing sperm whales, narwhals, belugas, beaked whales, oceanic dolphins, river dolphins, and porpoises. There are currently 72 species of odontocetes around the world; 17 are found in the northwest Atlantic and described in this book.

Teeth of odontocetes vary in form and function: the narwhal's tusk (top) is actually a tooth; the long-finned pilot whale (bottom) has pointed, peg-like teeth. *Marie Auger-Méthé (narwhal); Joana Augusto / Whitehead Lab, Dalhousie University (pilot whale)*

The suborder Odontoceti represents a diverse group of cetaceans in morphology and physiology, feeding behaviour, social behaviour, acoustic behaviour, movement patterns, and habitat preferences. In general, odontocetes are smaller than mysticetes, with the exception of the sperm whale. The world's smallest cetacean is the vaquita (*Phocoena sinus*), a porpoise, measuring only up to 1.5 metres in length. Along with northern hemisphere right whales, the vaquita is among the most critically endangered of all cetaceans; porpoises, in particular, are especially susceptible to bycatch, especially accidental entanglement in fishing gear and generally do not survive, even if they are rescued and set free. Harbour porpoises, the only porpoise in the northwest Atlantic, are also at high risk from entanglement. The sperm whale is the largest of all odontocetes, ranging up to 18 metres in length. It too is at risk from human fishing activities.

The teeth of odontocetes range in form and function. In most species, teeth function as normal feeding appendages—useful for catching, gripping, and manipulating their fish prey. In some species, however, teeth are not used for feeding. Many beaked whales have only one or two teeth (males only, females' teeth generally do not erupt) and, in some species, the teeth extrude from the bottom jaw and curve out and over the top of the whale's beak, impeding its ability to open its mouth more than several centimetres. The purpose of this is not well understood; it may aid in suction-feeding by limiting the opening diameter.

Beaked whales' teeth may also function as a secondary sexual organ, possibly for competing males battling to access a female. Most male beaked whales, some dolphins, and sperm whales display excessive scarring along their bodies, which may support this hypothesis. The narwhal's tusk is actually a tooth that may act as a sensory organ and as a secondary sexual characteristic.

Widely distributed, many species found in all ocean basins

Some species are popular in captivity (killer whales, bottlenose dolphins, belugas)

Most species are social and form stable or fluid groups from two to several hundred individuals

Vocalizations and echolocation are important for communicating and foraging

Have relatively large brains, asymmetrical skulls, and a "melon"; all three are thought to have evolved for acoustics and, especially, echolocation

Typically swim rapidly; some species often bow-ride and perform above-water aerobatics

Targeted during whaling operations, especially sperm whales and shore-driven dolphin fisheries

TAXONOMY

Kingdom: Animalia
Phylum: Chordata
Class: Mammalia

Order: Cetacea
Suborder: Odontoceti
10 families, 72 species

TOOTHED SPECIES

ADULT SIZE: 18 m (male); 12 m (female)

COLOUR: Dark grey to black or brownish

SPEED: Bursts up to 18-23 knots (33-43 km/h); typical travelling speed ~3-8 knots (6-15 km/h)

GROUP SIZE: Mature males typically solitary; immature males travel in "bachelor" groups of 2-3; females stay in maternal groups of ~12 individuals

PRIMARY FOOD: Cephalopods, specifically medium-sized squid

DISTINGUISHING CHARACTERISTICS: Large, square-shaped head; wrinkly skin from behind head to tail; offset blowhole makes angled blow forward and left; dorsal ridge instead of fin at tail stock; nearly always fluke-up in terminal dive

POPULATION STATUS: Vulnerable (IUCN 2008)

MORPHOLOGY: Adult head one-quarter to one-third total body length, composed mostly of a spermaceti organ, which may adjust buoyancy when diving

SEXUAL DIMORPHISM: Adult males about 30-50% longer than females and three times as heavy

BEHAVIOUR: Deep divers, to 3,200 m; can hold breath for 60 minutes

HISTORY: Can be aggressive when pursued, corroborated by well-documented accounts of sinking the large *Essex* and *Ann Alexander* ships

BRAIN SIZE: Largest brain of any animal

GENERATION TIME AND REPRODUCTIVE RATE: Estimated generation time 27 years; can live 70 years; females give birth every 3-6 years to single calf

SPERM WHALE
Physeter macrocephalus

Sperm whales are the largest members of the Odontoceti family and the largest toothed animal. Their French name *cachalot* is an archaic French word for "tooth" or "big teeth." The related Portuguese term is *cahola*, meaning "big head," which is also the translation for the Russian term *kashalot*. When they are seen at sea, sperm whales are difficult to confuse with other species; they have been described as "logs" floating at the surface.

Sperm whales have a wide distribution: from polar ice caps to the equator in both hemispheres. Although generally found at shelf edges in offshore regions and thought to inhabit deep-water canyon-type habitats, sperm whales reside in nearshore areas, such as inshore Newfoundland, and some partially enclosed seas, such as the Gulf of Mexico, Gulf of California, and the Mediterranean Sea. The behaviour and biology of this species has long interested researchers and mar-

1 METRE

iners and has also led to more than a few tall tales. Who has not tried to read a copy of Herman Melville's *Moby Dick*?

While sperm whales are distributed throughout the world, it is believed that only males travel to latitudes above 40° north and south. Females typically remain in tropical and subtropical waters, where they raise their calves. As is the case with all other large whale species, the sperm whale was subject to excessive whaling during open-boat and modern whaling for over 100 years. The oil in the whale's spermaceti organ, originally thought to contain its sperm, was the main target.

Spermaceti was used in candles, soaps, cosmetics, and machine oil. Ambergris, a waxy, grey to blackish solid substance produced in the sperm whale's digestive system and periodically regurgitated, was used in expensive perfume. The teeth, too, were valuable and often turned into scrimshaw, works of art by whalers on long voyages.

Distinguishing characteristics

Sperm whales are unlikely to be confused with other whale species at sea or from the air. They have a large head that appears squarish in profile. When they are viewed from above, they are thinner in width than in depth, giving them a submarine-like appearance. Their lower jaw holds 18 to 26 pairs of teeth, which fit into sockets in the top jaw.

Sperm whales are black to brown-grey and have a distinctive white outlining of their lower jaw and white colouration on their stomach. The skin on a sperm whale's head is relatively smooth, but the rest of its body is characterized by bumpy

A mature male sperm whale diving in the Gully, near Sable Island off Nova Scotia. *Marina Milligan / Whitehead Lab, Dalhousie University*

ATLANTIC CANADA AND NORTHEAST UNITED STATES 65

or wrinkled skin. Its blowhole is positioned at the front of its head, offset to the left. As a result, its low bushy blow is angled forward and to the left, which can be important in identification.

Sperm whales have a dorsal ridge instead of a dorsal fin close to the tail stock. The flukes are broad and triangular and feature a deep notch in the centre. Both the dorsal and ventral sides of the fluke are black, although white scarring may be present. When sperm whales dive, they raise their flukes out of the water. With the whale in this position, scientists can photograph the underside (ventral) surface of the fluke to identify individuals.

Male and female sperm whales are easily distinguished by size: they are among the most sexually dimorphic species on earth. Adult male sperm whales can be 30 to 50 per cent longer than adult females.

Feeding and behaviour

Sperm whales are deep divers, diving at least 3,200 metres, possibly more. They can hold their breath for an hour. Adult males, which are larger in mass and can therefore store more oxygen in their blood and muscle tissue, may hold their breath for up to two hours. Typical dives, however, last about 35 minutes.

These unique diving abilities result from the whales' feeding behaviour. Sperm whales feed predominantly on cephalopods. Although they may target giant squid, colossal squid, and octopi, medium-sized squid are the prey of choice. Sperm whales have also consumed fish, even taking fish directly off lines from fishing boats.

Like other odontocetes, sperm whales use echolocation to locate and identify prey. The spermaceti organ, in addition to playing a role in changing the whale's buoyancy during diving, may function in the production, emission, and/or reception of echolocation clicks. Some specific repeated patterns, "codas," may be acoustic signatures for individual or groups of sperm whales.

One of the most interesting facets of sperm whale behaviour occurs from birth through adolescence. Females typically stay in tropical or subtropical waters for the entirety of their lives, living in stable groups of about 12 adult females and their offspring. While female young tend not to leave their maternal group, males between the ages of 4 and 21 join bachelor groups. As males age, they tend to live solitarily in northern latitudes, only migrating to female groups during breeding seasons. Females reach sexual maturity between 7 to 13 years, males at 18.

Since the female and offspring groups are genetically related, a form of babysitting occurs among the mature members.

The sperm whale's low, bushy blow is angled to the left due to the position of its blowhole. *Marina Milligan / Whitehead Lab, Dalhousie University*

When a mother needs to dive for food, she may be away from the surface for up to an hour, leaving a baby that cannot yet accompany her to such depths. Another female will watch and protect the young at the surface. She may even feed another female's young if she is lactating. This remarkable process has recently been discovered and documented by scientists. Similar cooperative relationships are seen in other marine mammal species, such as killer whales, as well as terrestrial mammals, such as elephants, lions, and wolves.

The broad, black fluke of a sperm whale near St-Pierre-et-Miquelon as it begins a terminal dive. *Nadine and Thierry Vogenstahl*

Population status

Sperm whales are listed by the IUCN as Vulnerable. As a result of heavy whaling, sperm whale numbers dropped from about 1.1 million before widespread whaling began in the early eighteenth century to about 100,000 in 2012. In other words, sperm whales were reduced to an estimated 9 per cent of their original population. This is not dissimilar to the numbers for other whale species targeted during whaling.

The estimated maximum rate of population increase per year is 1 per cent. In some areas, however, populations are declining rather than increasing. As a result, sperm whales may not recover from the population depletion caused by whaling. Some biological factors (see Threats below) may cause the lack of recovery, as other great whale species, such as blue and fin whales, have shown population rebound.

Some sperm whale populations, such as those in the western North Atlantic, seem to be healthy, with positive reproduction figures.

Threats

Sperm whales are no longer heavily hunted. Many populations are far offshore in deep-water areas where human interactions are not yet a major threat, and few of their primary food sources are being commercially harvested.

Sperm whales are at greatest risk from habitat degradation, such as increasing ocean noise. As previously noted, sound is important in the feeding and social behaviour of sperm whales. Some populations have high levels of contaminants in their blubber. The effects of this on the whales' health require further study.

Entanglement in fishing gear such as gill-nets is a growing problem in some areas of the world. This has been documented to an alarming rate off Newfoundland and off the Labrador shelf. Hostility from fishers poses a threat—it is not uncommon for sperm whales to be shot. Some countries, such as Japan, actively hunt sperm whales, while others have done so until recently.

In some populations, such as the Antarctic and southeastern Pacific, the effects of whaling linger. For example, mature males were heavily exploited in Antarctica and females in other areas. This not only decreases reproduction rates but also breaks strong social bonds among females, especially by removing older matriarchal females.

TOOTHED SPECIES

ADULT SIZE: 8-9.5 m (male); 7-8.5 m (female)

COLOUR: Dark grey to brownish body with lighter underside

SPEED: Usually 2-3 knots (4-6 km/h) at the surface

GROUP SIZE: Solitary or groups of 1-4, occasionally up to 20 individuals

PRIMARY FOOD: Squid

DISTINGUISHING CHARACTERISTICS: Largest beaked whale in North Atlantic; large, bulbous melon and prominent beak; adult males: white face marked by scars

POPULATION STATUS: Data Deficient (IUCN 2008)

MORPHOLOGY: Two teeth in lower jaw, only erupt in adult males

SEXUAL DIMORPHISM: Adult males up to 25% larger than adult females; noticeably large and pronounced melon with more gently sloping beak-to-melon contour in adult males

NAME ORIGIN: Derived from Latin ampulla, meaning "bottle" or "flask," likely refers to beak or body shape

NORTHERN BOTTLENOSE WHALE
Hyperoodon ampullatus

Northern bottlenose whales are found only in the North Atlantic. The largest beaked whale in the region, they are the best studied of all beaked whales. Like other beaked whales, they are deep divers and are most commonly found near the continental shelf edge, typically in waters 500-1,500 metres deep, and often concentrated near submarine canyons, trenches, and gullies. They have, however, often been reported inshore in shallower waters around Newfoundland and along the Labrador shelf.

Northern bottlenose whales were one of the few beaked whale species targeted during the whaling era. Catch records point to at least six separate

1 METRE

areas of abundance: off Nova Scotia in the Gully, in northern Labrador and the Davis Strait, off northern Iceland, two isolated populations off Norway, and near Spitzbergen, Svalbard archipelago. It is possible that each region represents isolated stocks, as evidence of seasonal migrations between these areas has yet to be documented.

Nova Scotia's Gully population is the best studied. DNA evidence suggests that these whales, at least, are genetically distinct. They are also smaller and believed to breed at a different time of year than the nearby populations off Labrador and northern Iceland. Little is known about the central and western Atlantic populations.

Distinguishing characteristics

Northern bottlenose whales are robust, rotund toothed whales that are aptly named: they have a long, bottle-shaped snout that is distinct from their bulbous forehead. The beak slopes more gently to the melon on juveniles and adult females; adult males' foreheads are steeper and even bulge upward and appear more square than round when they are viewed from the side. The head and face of both sexes lighten with age. The melons of adult males can become nearly white and are often marked with scars from interactions with other northern bottlenose males.

A brownish or yellowish head on some individuals is actually a thin covering of

A group of northern bottlenose dolphins swimming alongside the research vessel. *Whitehead Lab, Dalhousie University*

The curved, relatively small dorsal fin of a northern bottlenose whale. Scars are common on most adults. *Whitehead Lab, Dalhousie University*

diatoms (a single-celled algae) and is not a true colour or patterning. Further, scarring along the body, predominantly on males, typically increases with age. The overall body colour of adults ranges from dark grey to brownish with a lighter underside. Calves are darker than adults and can be black to brown.

Bottlenose whales have two teeth in the lower jaw, although these erupt through the gum only in mature males. Unerupted vestigial teeth can occur in both upper and lower jaws. Male and female bottlenose whales have two angled, forward-pointing throat pleats. Their curved dorsal fins are small relative to their body size and are located far back along the body. The pectoral fins are relatively small and the flukes typically lack a central notch.

Beaked whales are difficult to distinguish at sea, and northern bottlenose whales are no exception. Their distribution overlaps with that of several other beaked whales in Atlantic Canadian waters. Most often, the head shape, body colour, and body size identify northern bottlenose whales.

Feeding and behaviour

The primary prey of northern bottlenose whales is squid from the genus *Gonatus*, although they may sometimes take herring and redfish. They are capable of reaching depths of 1,400 or more metres. Much of their feeding occurs at or near the bottom. They can remain underwater for at least an hour.

Typically northern bottlenose whales are seen in groups of two to four, although **larger groups of up to 20** have been recorded, **as have solitary** individuals. As with other **deep-diving cetaceans**, northern bottlenose **whales use** sound not only for **communication** and socializing but also to find their **prey in deep waters and in the dark.** Their easily identifiable echolocation clicks are important to understanding their ecology and behaviour. Whistles and chirps believed to originate from bottlenose whales have been recorded in the 3-16 kHz range.

Population status

It is thought that at least 30 per cent of the population of northern bottlenose whales was taken during whaling. Full recovery is not considered probable.

Long-term studies suggest that, although the global population has been depleted, the population trend is stable, as neither

The whale's bottle-shaped snout is distinct from its forehead. *Whitehead Lab, Dalhousie University*

A group of northern bottlenose whales in the Gully, near Sable Island off Nova Scotia. *Kristin O'Brien / Whitehead Lab, Dalhousie University*

significant gains nor significant losses to the Atlantic population have been observed for at least 15 years. The species is currently listed as Data Deficient, although subpopulations, such as that at the Gully, appear at risk.

Threats

Northern bottlenose whales face the same risks as other whales and dolphins, such as habitat degradation. As is the case with most deep-diving species, northern bottlenose whales are at risk to anthropogenic sounds. In particular, they are sensitive to naval sonar and seismic surveys, which put high source level sounds into the ocean. This noise interferes with their acoustic environment for communication and feeding. Loud sounds can damage sensitive tissue, leading to deafness and possibly death. Based on an examination of dead individuals, it has been hypothesized that loud underwater sounds may also force deep-diving whales to retreat to the surface as quickly as possible. When a whale surfaces quickly from depth, the rapid change in pressure (from high pressure in deep water to low pressure at the surface) causes nitrogen gas in the bloodstream to form bubbles. In humans, these bubbles collect in and around the joints and cause what divers know as the "bends." A similar process can occur in whales and may lead to death.

A northern bottlenose whale leaping out of the water in the Gully. *Catalina Gomez / Whitehead Lab, Dalhousie University*

ATLANTIC CANADA AND NORTHEAST UNITED STATES

TOOTHED SPECIES

ADULT SIZE: 7.5 m (male); 7 m (female)

COLOUR: Adults dark grey to light rusty brown; head and back lighten nearly to white as they age

SPEED: Over 7 knots (13 km/h) at surface; 1-3 knots (2-6 km/h) between dives

GROUP SIZE: 2-7, rarely encountered alone

PRIMARY FOOD: Deep-sea squid

DISTINGUISHING CHARACTERISTICS: Rounder face and unpronounced, shorter jaw than other beaked whales; white head (adults); older adult males have a lighter back and head

POPULATION STATUS: Least Concern (IUCN 2008)

DISTRIBUTION: Most widely distributed of all beaked whale species, from Arctic to Antarctica; specific habitat preference: depths of 1,500-3,500 m, steep bottom relief, and surface temperatures >10°C

DIVING ABILITY: Up to 40 minutes and >1,100 m

COMMON NAME: "Goose-beaked whales," as head in profile resembles that of a goose

CUVIER'S BEAKED WHALE
Ziphius cavirostris

Cuvier's beaked whales have the largest distribution of all beaked whales: in every ocean basin, many enclosed seas, and range from the tropics to lower polar latitudes. Research indicates that this species prefers regions with ocean surface temperatures greater than 10°C and ocean depths greater than 200 metres, although they most commonly occur in areas with depths between 1,500 and 3,500 metres. Because of this, Cuvier's beaked whales in the northwest Atlantic are likely limited to south of Newfoundland and the Gulf of St. Lawrence and offshore at the shelf break, possibly in relation to the warmer Gulf Stream current.

Until the early 2000s, information about Cuvier's beaked whales was based primarily on information gathered from stranded individuals. As is the case with

every beaked whale species, Cuvier's beaked whales are difficult to discern from others in the family Ziphiidae and are rarely at the surface for long periods of time. As a result, most multi-species whale and dolphin surveys, whether conducted from aircraft or vessel, are unable to provide confident abundance estimates or range distribution of this species. Cuvier's and other beaked whales are usually categorized as "unidentified" species during surveys since they are so hard to sight and distinguish.

Distinguishing characteristics

Cuvier's beaked whales are among the most difficult species to properly identify, or encounter, of the whales and dolphins of the northwest Atlantic. Their body colour can range from dark grey to light rust or reddish brown. Individuals may have a speckled appearance, especially on the belly and ventral side of the tail stock. These white, oval marks are scars likely caused by cookie-cutter sharks or lampreys. Linear white or grey scars may also be visible, predominantly on males and likely caused by other males, possibly a result of competition among males to gain access to a female.

This is not uncommon among toothed cetaceans.

In general, Cuvier's beaked whales have a robust, relatively rotund body shape compared to that of most beaked whales. Their beak is also comparatively short, which creates a more bulbous melon. The melon slopes relatively steeply to the beak and is not differentiated from it. Adult Cuvier's have a white or

A surfacing adult male Cuvier's beaked whale. *Robin W. Baird / cascadiaresearch.org*

A group of at least three Cuvier's beaked whales near Hawaii.
Robin W. Baird / cascadiaresearch.org

cream-coloured head and face; this is more pronounced in males and, as they age, their back, from the head to dorsal fin, whitens. The dorsal fin is small and varies from sharply hooked to nearly triangular and is set about two-thirds back along the body. Mature males erupt two forward and upwardly pointing teeth at the front tip of their lower jaw. These are visible when the mouth is closed and are likely a secondary sexual characteristic.

The rounded facial shape and short jaw of Cuvier's beaked whales may aid identification. Mature males may be identified by their white backs. Cuvier's beaked whales may be mistaken for northern bottlenose whales; the latter are larger and mature males have a more bulbous and steep melon and pronounced beak.

Feeding and behaviour

Cuvier's beaked whales, like most deep-diving cetaceans, prefer squid, although they may also feed on fish and some crustaceans. They are thought to feed at the ocean's bottom as well as in the water column. Neither males nor females have functional teeth and presumably eat prey at close range by suction.

Cuvier's beaked whales are usually observed in groups of two to seven individuals but are also seen alone. Their dives typically last between 20 and 40 minutes and can reach depths exceeding 1,100 metres. Their blow is low, diffuse, pointed slightly forward and to the left, and usually difficult to see.

Population status

There are no worldwide abundance estimates for Cuvier's beaked whales. Based on localized surveys, it is estimated that there are over 100,000 worldwide. This suggests that they may be the most abundant of all beaked whales. They are listed by the IUCN as Least Concern. Based on recent genetic analyses of some populations in different oceans, it does not appear likely that individuals move between ocean basins.

The speckled appearance of some adult Cuvier's beaked whales is caused by scarring. *Robin W. Baird / cascadiaresearch.org*

An adult Cuvier's beaked whale. The white oval-shaped scars are likely caused by cookie-cutter sharks or lampreys. *Robin W. Baird / cascadiaresearch.org*

Threats

A small number of Cuvier's beaked whales are killed every year due to entanglement or accidental capture in fishing gear. In the western North Atlantic, bycatch rates appear to be low, however, with only one reported incident between 1994 and 1998.

Cuvier's beaked whales were never targeted during commercial whaling, although they are occasionally taken in the Pacific as direct catch. The number of Cuvier's beaked whales hunted each year is low and not a significant threat to the population. Japan, for example, takes between 3 and 35 a year.

The effects of other specific threats, such as overfishing prey fish and climate change, are unknown.

The greatest threat to Cuvier's beaked whales and all other deep-diving cetaceans is loud underwater noise, particularly naval sonar and seismic explorations. At least four mass stranding events between 1996 and 2002 are thought to have been connected with nearby naval sonar exercises. Loud underwater sounds cause Cuvier's beaked whales to flee at speeds of over 7 knots (13 km/h) from the source while at the surface. If the whale is deep underwater, loud sounds cause it to rapidly ascend, causing a condition similar to divers' bends, where gases such as nitrogen in the blood form bubbles that concentrate in joints and other areas of the body.

Although more research is warranted, it is known that Cuvier's beaked whales are susceptible to stranding; more conservation measures are needed for this species.

TOOTHED SPECIES

ADULT SIZE: 6.7 m (male); 5.7 (female)

COLOUR: Dark grey to jet black with anchor-shaped white patch on throat; grey cape behind dorsal fin

SPEED: Average 0.1-7.8 knots (0.2-14 km/h)

GROUP SIZE: 8-20; pods averaging 110 are common; herds up to 1,200 individuals have existed

PRIMARY FOOD: Squid and various fish species

DISTINGUISHING CHARACTERISTICS: Dark grey or black; large, round, bulbous melon above short beak; robust, long, low profile; hooked dorsal fin more prominent in adult males; long, narrow, tapered pectoral fins

POPULATION STATUS: Data Deficient (IUCN 2008)

REPRODUCTION: Gestation about 12 months; calves nurse up to 2 years; reproductive interval, 3 to 5 years; although pregnancy after 40 is rare, they have occurred up to 55; like killer whales, females undergo menopause and cannot reproduce

SUBPOPULATIONS: Two distinct geographically isolated subpopulations, North Atlantic and southern hemisphere circum-Antarctic, may warrant recognition as separate subspecies or even separate species; a third, the western North Pacific, is extinct

NAME ORIGIN: From long pectoral fins; called pilot whales as all group or pod members thought to follow one whale (pilot), even ashore, if stranded; species name *melas* is Greek for "black"; "pothead" and "blackfish," common names in eastern Canada, based on morphology and colouration

LONG-FINNED PILOT WHALE
Globicephala melas

Long-finned pilot whales are relatively well known and recognizable in Atlantic Canadian waters because of their abundance, highly gregarious and social nature, and association with squid fisheries. While there are two species of pilot whales (long-finned and short-finned, *G. macrorhynchus*) worldwide, only the long-finned pilot whale (referred to as "pilot whale" in this chapter) is found in the northwest Atlantic, extending to the subarctic waters of northern Labrador.

The pilot whale is typically an oceanic and deep-diving cetacean restricted to a habitat temperature range of 0°-25°C. Although most abundant at or past the continental shelf edge, they are also observed inshore, most often where deep ocean contours reach the shoreline. Its distribution matches that of its preferred prey, squid and other pelagic cephalopods.

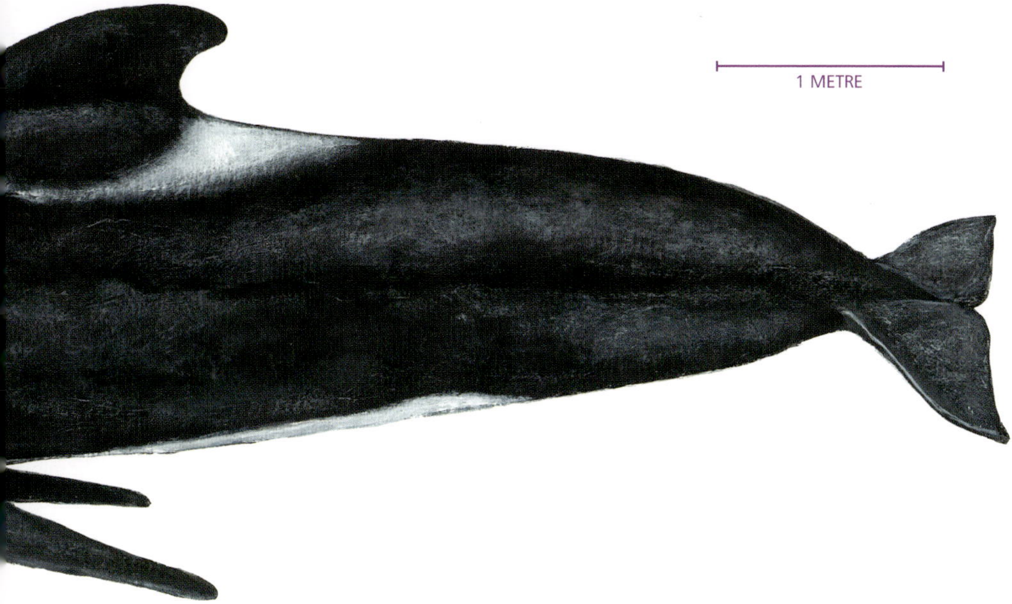

The migration pattern of pilot whales in the northwest Atlantic is linked to their reproductive behaviour and cycle. In general, they are distributed near the shelf edge near the southern limits of their range (northeast and mid-Atlantic US latitudes) from mid-winter through early spring. They then travel north, past the outer edges of the Gulf of Maine and Georges Bank to Nova Scotia, finally arriving in Newfoundland in the summer, where they remain until late fall and early winter.

Pilot whales were intensely hunted during the Newfoundland drive fishery from 1947 to 1971. In this fishery, whales were driven ashore en masse, usually into an enclosed bay with no escape route, and killed. These whales were used for meat, pet food, oil, and/or fertilizer. The tight social bonds among pilot whale groups works against this species and they will not separate—if one member of the pod is forced ashore, the others stay with this individual. These social bonds result in mass strandings of entire herds of pilot whales.

Although pilot whales were hunted around the Faroe Islands, northeast United States, Greenland, Iceland, Scotland, Japan, and elsewhere, the Newfoundland fishery was the most extreme, taking so many whales that it ended with a severely depleted stock. Nearly 4,000 pilot whales were taken in Newfoundland on average each year between 1950 and 1959. In 1956 alone, close to 10,000 were driven ashore and killed. A decreasing

The long-finned pilot whale's bulbous melon and broad, hooked dorsal fin are distinguishing features. *Nadine and Thierry Vogenstahl*

An adult and calf pilot whale in Pleasant Bay, Cape Breton, Nova Scotia. *Joana Augusto / Whitehead Lab, Dalhousie University*

population led to decreasing catches: close to 1,500 were taken on average per year from 1960 to 1969. It is estimated that over 54,000 pilot whales were taken during the Newfoundland drive fishery, which substantially altered and reduced the local population.

Distinguishing characteristics

Pilot whales range in colour from dark brown or dark grey to jet black. It has a white or light grey saddle patch behind the dorsal fin; a white or light grey blaze behind the eye may not be visible on northern hemisphere pilot whales. Visibility of these markings often varies between individuals and by at-sea light or atmospheric conditions. Its belly is white and it has an anchor-shaped patch on its throat, visible when it spyhops.

The pilot whale's body is relatively long and robust. Its long, narrow, and tapered or pointed pectoral fins are approximately one-third the length of its body. The dorsal fin, positioned forward of the midline of the body, is large and hooked with an elongated baseline. The dorsal fin on adult males is even more large and pronounced. The whale's melon is round and bulbous, sometimes protruding forward of its mouth, and is more pronounced in adult males than in adult females or juveniles. The pilot whale has a short beak.

Pilot whales may be confused with other small cetaceans in the northwest Atlantic, including killer whales, minke whales, and bottlenose dolphins. Observations of the dorsal fin shape, melon and beak shape, and body colour are usually sufficient for correct identification. South of the northwest Atlantic, the distribution of short-finned pilot whales overlaps with the long-finned species and are nearly impossible to identify at sea.

Feeding and behaviour

Pilot whales predominantly feed on squid and other pelagic cephalopods. Their preferred prey in the northwest Atlantic is short-finned squid, but they have also taken medium-sized fish species such as mackerel, cod, turbot, herring, hake, and dogfish. Pilot whales feed mainly at night as squid travel up the water column as part of their daily vertical migration cycle. In some areas where the prey has been overfished and depleted, once-abundant pilot whales become rare. Pilot whales can dive for over 18 minutes and to at least 828 metres.

Pilot whales produce a variety of sounds, including tonal calls, whistles, and echolocation clicks. Their vocalizations, especially the whistles among groups active at the surface, can be heard above the water. Their whistles, which range from 1 kHz to 8 kHz, are believed to help coordinate behaviour, especially during feeding. Research on pilot whale vocalizations is advancing, including focal populations

A long-finned pilot whale off Nova Scotia. *Joana Augusto / Whitehead Lab, Dalhousie University*

within Atlantic Canada, such as the population in and around St. Lawrence Bay off Cape Breton Island, Nova Scotia.

Pilot whale social behaviour is also being studied. The nucleus of pilot whale society is the small, close-knit group comprised of genetically related whales and likely structured around a female and her offspring. In general, groups[1] signified by close, long-term bonds among whales have an average membership of 8 to 20 individuals. Pods or schools, averaging

Pilot whales near Cape Spear, Newfoundland and Labrador. *Tara S. Stevens / DFO*

A young pilot whale. *Joana Augusto / Whitehead Lab, Dalhousie University*

110 individuals, are the gathering of several groups and likely contain some form of social or familial bonds. Herds of up to 1,200 whales have been observed. Herds may be scattered over a wide geographic area and composed of many groups, a collection of pods, or some other combination. Large gatherings of more than 1,000 individuals are rare.

Population status

No confident worldwide abundance estimate or population trend for the pilot whale exists. Based on an amalgamation of several survey estimates, some dating from the late 1980s and none more recent than 1994, there may be nearly 1 million pilot whales globally. However, they are considered Data Deficient (2008) due to a lack of recent and reliable data.

A published 2006 population assessment estimated the pilot whale population of the northwest Atlantic, which includes mid-United States latitudes, to be approximately 31,000 individuals. This figure is likely inflated, as both pilot whale species were counted and not differentiated where their distribution overlaps. A 1980s abundance estimate suggested the population off eastern Newfoundland was approximately 13,000. The pre-drive fishery estimate was in the range of 50,000 to 60,000 individuals.

Threats

Although the Newfoundland drive fishery for pilot whales closed after the whales were decimated, active fisheries for this species still exist in Greenland and the Faroe Islands. Few pilot whales

A pilot whale spyhopping. *Joana Augusto / Whitehead Lab, Dalhousie University*

are taken each year, however, and catch levels are believed to be far below what could cause stock depletion. Out of a population of approximately 100,000 whales around the Faroe Islands, for example, only an average of 850 individuals are taken yearly. The Greenland fishery is even smaller.

Threats common to many other cetaceans have a greater effect on pilot whales: excessive levels of underwater noise, such as that made by naval sonar and seismic exploration; incidental catches, or bycatch, in various fisheries; entanglement in fishing gear; and overfishing of prey species, leading to a shortage of food. Incidental catches, which are likely underreported, and competition with fisheries, particularly squid, are probably the greatest threats to pilot whales. Global climate change, pollution, and disease likely also affect these whales.

More attention must be given to this species' interaction with fisheries, especially for those whales which undertake migrations that cross national borders.

---

1. Researchers use and define terms such as "group," "pod," "school," and "herd" differently and sometimes interchangeably. For some species, such as killer whales, sperm whales, and pilot whales, with socially driven life patterns, these terms are significantly different and refer to specific social behaviour or relations depending on whether members are considered part of a group, pod, school, or herd.

TOOTHED SPECIES

ADULT SIZE: 6 m (male); 5.5 m (female)

COLOUR: Jet black body with well-defined white markings; saddle patch is usually light grey and diffuse

SPEED: Up to 26 knots (48 km/h); likely second fastest marine mammal; typical travelling speed 2-5 knots (4-9 km/h)

GROUP SIZE: Adult males solitary and in groups; in Atlantic Canadian waters 2-20 or more; average group size is 3-7

PRIMARY FOOD: Subpopulations of killer whales target different prey but usually fish or marine mammal eaters

DISTINGUISHING CHARACTERISTICS: Black and white colouration; tall, broad, triangular dorsal fin in adult males, shorter, more curved fin in females and juvenile males

POPULATION STATUS: Data Deficient (IUCN 2008)

TAXONOMY: Member of dolphin family

LIFESPAN: Males up to 50-60 years; females, 80-90 years

REPRODUCTION: Gestation 15-18 months; in some well-studied populations (e.g., off British Columbia) it is thought that healthy female's calving interval is one calf every 5 years; solid foods introduced early but some calves not fully weaned until 2 years

KILLER WHALE
Orcinus orca

The killer whale is a large, social carnivore occupying both near-shore and offshore areas worldwide. It is the largest member of the dolphin family and its black and white colouration makes it easily identifiable at sea. Killer whales are popular tourist attractions at aquariums and they have had starring roles in Hollywood movies (*Free Willy*, *Orca*). Due to popular culture exposure, killer whales are recognizable even by those who have never seen the ocean.

1 METRE

As a cosmopolitan species, some populations of killer whales are relatively well studied; others, such as those in the northwest Atlantic, remain undocumented. Much of the research on this species' ecology and behaviour is based on studies in the northeast Pacific. Recently, killer whales in Antarctica, Norway, the United Kingdom, Russia, and New Zealand have been the subject of demographic and behavioural studies in an attempt to reveal similarities and differences with the better-known British Columbia populations. As a result, worldwide knowledge of this species is increasing, with the exception of lower-density populations or those in difficult-to-access areas, such

An adult female killer whale, showing a much shorter and curved dorsal fin than the adult male. Juvenile males likewise have shorter, curved dorsal fins before sexual maturity and are commonly confused with females at sea. *Illustration by Trish Stevens*

A male killer whale swimming alongside the research vessel, his large, triangular dorsal fin and saddle patch in profile. *Tara S. Stevens / DFO*

Distinguishing characteristics

Killer whales are perhaps the most easily identifiable of whales and dolphins. Both male and female killer whales have unmistakable colouration: black with a white patch behind each eye, a grey saddle patch behind the dorsal fin, and a contrasting white ventral surface extending from the lower jaw to the tail stock. White lobes extend up and along its flank. The undersides of the fluke and pectoral flippers are white.

as the northwest Atlantic. To fill this gap, research is currently being conducted in the northwest Atlantic, mostly off Newfoundland and Labrador, but also throughout the rest of Atlantic Canada and the northeast United States.

Killer whales in the northeast Pacific are divided into three distinct subpopulations: residents, transients, and offshore. These groups overlap in range and distribution but are sexually isolated (do not breed together). Their behaviour and physical characteristics are distinct. For example, residents eat only fish (in particular, Chinook salmon), while transients eat only marine mammals (mostly seals but also some whale and dolphin species). The diet of offshore killer whales may include shark and some fish species. Group size and composition, vocal behaviour, and movement patterns differ among the subpopulations or ecotypes. These three ecotypes of killer whales even look different, with differently proportioned dorsal fins and body sizes.

Research on whales near Antarctica indicates that there are four killer whale subpopulations. Although all killer whales are currently recognized as one species, some researchers have suggested dividing them into separate species or subspecies to account for their differences.

Killer whales have large, erect dorsal fins. Adult male dorsal fins can reach nearly 2 metres, are triangular, and may have a slight bend either forward or backward; females have a much shorter and curved fin. Juvenile males also have short, curved fins and can be confused with females until they reach maturity. These standards, like colouration, vary among ecotypes and individuals.

When these whales are viewed from behind, the dorsal fins of older adult males are commonly wavy, which increases with age. In other adults, a completely slumped over fin can signal disease or other ailment; the exact cause of this remains unknown.

A killer whale's distinct black and white patterning. Note the white eye patch and blunt, non-discrete beak. *Tara S. Stevens / DFO*

A group of at least six killer whales ranging in age from a young calf to juvenile to adult. The white patterning of especially young calves often has an orange tint.
Nadine and Thierry Vogenstahl

Due to their large, dark dorsal fins, pilot whales, Risso's dolphins, and white-beaked dolphins may be confused with killer whales. Confusion would most likely originate from distance or poor sighting conditions.

Feeding and behaviour

Killer whales feed on a variety of prey and, as a species, are considered generalists. It is well documented that some subpopulations prefer particular types of prey (e.g., marine mammal versus fish), and even certain species (e.g., Chinook salmon).

Around the world, killer whales prey upon seals, dolphins, minke whales, tuna, salmon, small schooling fish (e.g., herring or capelin), sharks, and rays. Attacks on seabirds and sea turtles have been witnessed, although these are not considered a substantial part of the diet. Killer whales have been observed killing larger cetacean species, such as humpback whales, although this is rare, partly due to the risk to the killer whales themselves. Killer whales are at the top of the food chain and they are not known to have any natural predators.

Killer whale feeding behaviour interests many researchers. Different populations employ specific tactics for attacking and killing their prey. Killer whales learn and perfect certain predation tactics, which are then taught to offspring and passed along generations. Certain groups of whales perfect foraging tactics for particular species. For example, some populations of killer whales may beach themselves to catch fleeing seals. Others

An adult male killer whale. Note the ripples in the trailing edge of his dorsal fin, a characteristic that develops as males age. *Nadine and Thierry Vogenstahl*

use cooperative feeding methods to corral schooling fish or to take larger prey.

Population status

Killer whales are listed as Data Deficient by the IUCN, although some subpopulations in the northeast Pacific are considered Endangered and at high risk of extinction. The worldwide population is approximately 50,000, although this is likely an underestimate as data for many parts of the world are unavailable. This abundance estimate amalgamates all killer whales.

Killer whales are most often found in high-latitude, nearshore waters of high productivity. In the Antarctic, for example, densities appear to be higher near the ice edge, where groups of tens to hundreds have been observed. Similar-sized groups have been seen near the British Isles and in other areas of the world, although smaller group sizes are generally more common.

It is believed that, due to the threats described below, a global killer whale population reduction of up to 30 per cent within three generations, or about 77 years, may be likely.

Threats

Killer whales were captured during the modern whaling period, although they were a low-target species. They were generally considered a nuisance and competition to whaling activities and, therefore, were often shot, killed, and left at sea. Killer whales are still taken in small-scale coastal fisheries in Japan, Greenland, Indonesia, and some Caribbean islands. Only small numbers are captured, and the effect on local populations in these areas remains unknown.

Killer whales are still considered competition to fisheries around the world and are often targeted and shot. Depredation of long-line fisheries exists in many areas and is an increasing problem, especially in Alaska. Killer whales have been seen in the vicinity of fishing activities in Atlantic Canada and the northeast United States, although there are no known reports of intentional shootings. Bycatch in fishing operations is rare for this species. Live captures of killer whales for public display in aquariums is much less frequent than it was in the past.

Habitat degradation is a major threat and includes exposure to contaminants that may bioaccumulate, behavioural disturbances from whale-watching activities, and large-scale reductions in particular prey species. Killer whales which frequent British Columbia's coastal waters, including at least one transient and two resident subpopulations, have such high PCB concentrations that the whales themselves are considered toxic. This can lead to immune and reproductive deficiencies.

Killer whales are highly social and vocal. Because their vocalizations are used for communication and foraging, the introduction of excessive noise from whale-watching vessels can interfere with the whale's natural behaviour. Physical disruption from vessels in the location of certain groups of killer whales can also affect foraging and social behaviour and increase the risk of injury from collisions.

Drastic declines in marine mammal populations and the collapse of important fish stocks from over-fishing threaten the killer whale's food supply. Although killer whales are highly intelligent and display adaptive foraging tactics, they will not deviate from their usual prey. For example, killer whales that prey on Chinook salmon in the northeast Pacific are at risk after the collapse of the Chinook salmon stock, and those in the Strait of Gibraltar are at risk of extinction due to the depletion of the Mediterranean blue fin tuna.

A juvenile killer whale, displaying many scars and scratches from other killer whales on its saddle patch and flank. This photo is a perfect identification/catalogue image as it captures the left side dorsal fin and saddle patch region.
Tara S. Stevens / DFO

TOOTHED SPECIES

ADULT SIZE: 5.5 m (male); 5.1 m (female)

COLOUR: Dark or slate grey topside; light grey underside

SPEED: Unavailable

GROUP SIZE: Possibly up to 8-10 individuals

PRIMARY FOOD: Squid

DISTINGUISHING CHARACTERISTICS: Longer jaw than other beaked whales in the northwest Atlantic; adult males have two triangular teeth on bottom jaw located posterior of beak tip

POPULATION STATUS: Data Deficient (IUCN 2008)

DISTRIBUTION: Most northerly species of *Mesoplodon* genus; exclusively in North Atlantic, mostly above latitude 30° north

EXTRALIMITAL SIGHTINGS: Few strandings and sightings in Mediterranean Sea and Gulf of Mexico, outside usual range

NAME ORIGIN: First living species of the Ziphiidae family described; originally believed two teeth characterized species (*bidens* "two" [*bi-*] "teeth" [*dens*]) but lower jaw of all whales in genus *Mesoplodon*, as well as other beaked whale species, have two teeth in lower jaw

SOWERBY'S BEAKED WHALE
Ziphius cavirostris

Sowerby's beaked whales, like many of its beaked whale relatives, are poorly understood. Much of what is known about this species is based on analysis of stranded specimens or from what is already known about other species in the *Mesoplodon* genus. Sowerby's beaked whales are exclusive to the North Atlantic, ranging on the east from the mid-United States seaboard to mid-Labrador regions.

Sowerby's beaked whales are among the most northerly distributed of all beaked whales, likely preferring deep water seaward of the continental shelf edge. Of the beaked whales, Sowerby's are the most commonly stranded and yet also least frequently recorded at sea.

88 WHALES AND DOLPHINS

1 METRE

Distinguishing characteristics

Sowerby's beaked whales' body shape is similar to that of other *Mesoplodons*: robust at the middle and tapering evenly at both ends to the tail and head. The dorsal fin is small, falcate, and positioned behind the middle of the back. These whales have a variable, though still visible, bulging melon in front of the blowhole. Their beak is fairly long and slender. Two teeth on either side of the lower jaw at its median (as opposed to at the tip for other *Mesoplodons*) erupt in mature males, are distinctively triangular in shape, and are visible when the mouth is closed. As with other species in this genus, their teeth are not used for foraging.

The body colour of Sowerby's beaked whales is relatively plain and countershaded. They have a dark or slate grey topside and light grey ventral surface. Their dorsal fin, pectoral flippers, and fluke are dark grey; the area around their eyes may also be darkened. Often, long, linear scars, either white or grey, are visible most typically on males. Round or oval white or grey spots may be present, primarily on younger Sowerby's beaked whales.

In the northwest Atlantic, Sowerby's beaked whales overlap in distribution with Cuvier's, True's, and Blainville's beaked whales. It may be impossible to differentiate between females and young whales of these species as they have similar shape and colour and less pronounced

The long, linear scars on this Sowerby's beaked whale were likely caused by interactions with other Sowerby's beaked whales. *Whitehead Lab / Dalhousie University*

proportions than adult males. Cuvier's beaked whales have a rounder face and short beak, and True's have a medium-length beak; adult males of both Cuvier's and True's beaked whales have two teeth at the front tip of their lower jaw. Although mature male Blainville's beaked whales have lower jaw teeth positioned far back from the front tip, their jaw is highly arched upward compared to that of Sowerby's. Despite these differences, it may be impossible to identify beaked whales at sea.

Feeding and behaviour

Sowerby's beaked whales are likely deep-diving whales. The few sightings that have positively identified Sowerby's at sea were in water 550 to 1,500 metres deep. Based on isotope analysis and examinations of stomach contents from stranded individuals, researchers have determined that Sowerby's feed on squid and fish, especially Atlantic cod.

Sowerby's are believed to occur in groups of 8 to 10 individuals, although this is based on scant evidence and may not represent the entire population. The largest mass stranding recorded was a group of six.

Sowerby's beaked whales can dive for 28 minutes, although this is likely an underestimate of this species' capabilities. Several reports have indicated that, upon surfacing, Sowerby's beaked whales break the water with their heads, becoming fully exposed at a steep angle. Little else is known about their biology and ecology.

Population status

Sowerby's beaked whales are listed by the IUCN as Data Deficient. Little is known about their population biology, and no global or regional abundance estimates exist.

Threats

Little is known about specific threats to

Sowerby's beaked whales photographed in the Gully, near Sable Island, off Nova Scotia. *Whitehead Lab / Dalhousie University*

Sowerby's beaked whales often break through the water's surface with their heads at a sharp angle. *Whitehead Lab / Dalhousie University*

Sowerby's beaked whales. They have been subject to incidental kills by whalers in Newfoundland, Iceland, and the Barents Sea (located north of Scandinavia and Russia and south of the Svalbard Islands, Norway). Some entanglements and bycatch in pelagic drift gill-nets set at the continental shelf edge from the Gulf of Maine to south of Cape Cod have been reported. Twenty-four Sowerby's beaked whales were caught between 1989 and 1998, although this particular fishery has since closed.

Like other beaked whales, Sowerby's are likely most at risk to entanglement in fishing gear and loud anthropogenic sound such as naval sonar and seismic exploration practices. The degree to which these threats affect Sowerby's beaked whales is not well known, but it does impact similar beaked whale populations.

Oceanographic and environmental changes that result from climate change may affect this species, although the nature and level of this impact is unclear.

The small, hooked dorsal fin of a Sowerby's beaked whale. Many scars are also visible. *Whitehead Lab / Dalhousie University*

TOOTHED SPECIES

ADULT SIZE: 5 m

COLOUR: Medium grey topside and lighter underside

SPEED: Unavailable

GROUP SIZE: Unavailable

PRIMARY FOOD: Squid

DISTINGUISHING CHARACTERISTICS: Moderately pronounced melon, medium-length jaw, and slightly curved mouth line; likely confused with Cuvier's and Blainville's beaked whales

POPULATION STATUS: Data Deficient (IUCN 2008)

DISTRIBUTION: Prefer temperate waters and avoid tropics, possibly separating them into northern and southern subspecies; substantiated by colour and morphologic differences

MORPHOLOGY: Narrow tail stock with pronounced ridge from dorsal fin to fluke

NAME ORIGIN: American biologist Frederick True chose species name *mirus*, meaning "wonderful"

TRUE'S BEAKED WHALE
Ziphius cavirostris

Very little is known about True's beaked whales. What is known about them is from the examination of dead, stranded individuals. It was believed until 1959 that True's beaked whales only occurred in the North Atlantic, until a specimen was discovered in South Africa. Based on stranding records, these whales appear to prefer temperate waters in both hemispheres and are not known to occur in the tropics within 30° north and south of the equator. The extent of stranding and sighting records ranges from Cape Breton, Nova Scotia, to the Bahamas.

Most of our knowledge about this species is based on genus-level characterizations. What is known about different species within the *Mesoplodon* genus is considered as likely for True's beaked whales.

Distinguishing characteristics

True's beaked whale is another rotund beaked whale that is gently tapered

1 METRE

Male True's beaked whale.

toward both tail and head. The melon appears as a slight pronounced bulge above its medium-sized beak. An adult male has two erupted teeth at the forward tip of the lower jaw, similar to those of Cuvier's beaked whales. The dorsal fin is relatively small and varies among individuals from curved to triangular. The dorsal fin is much darker than the back, which is light to medium grey. The fluke, lips, and circular patches around the eyes are also dark, while the length of the whale's underside is lighter.

In the northeast Atlantic, True's beaked whales can be confused with both Cuvier's and Blainville's beaked whales. Cuvier's have a much blunter face with a shorter beak; Blainville's, a flatter melon and an arched jawline. Identifying this species at sea is difficult.

Feeding and behaviour

Based on similar species' behaviour, it is believed that the main prey for True's beaked whales is deep-water squid, as analysis of the stomach contents of stranded specimens has revealed squid. True's beaked whales may take some fish as well, but this, too, remains unsubstantiated. It is only assumed, based on other related beaked whales, that True's beaked whales are a pelagic and deep-water species. Stable isotope analysis in one study suggested that these whales feed at a lower level of the food chain than Cuvier's and northern bottlenose whales, indicating that True's prefer smaller prey. Additional studies are warranted.

Since this species has rarely been identified at sea, little else is known about their behaviour, reproduction, and foraging habits.

Population status

There is no abundance estimate or population trend available for True's beaked whales. The species is, however, considered rare in Canadian waters based on stranding statistics. They are listed as Data Deficient by the IUCN.

Threats

No threats to this species have been confirmed and there is no evidence that they have ever been hunted. Based on data for similar species, entanglement in fishing gear such as deep-water gill-nets, and loud noise from naval exercises and seismic exploration are the most probable threats.

TOOTHED SPECIES

ADULT SIZE: 4.7 m (male); 4 m (female)

COLOUR: Mottled or spotted black and white topside with whiter belly, becoming whiter all over with age

SPEED: Typical travelling speed <3 knots (6 km/h)

GROUP SIZE: Solitary, or groups of 2-20; herds of hundreds of individuals can form

PRIMARY FOOD: Fish, especially Greenland halibut and Arctic cod, squid, and shrimp

DISTINGUISHING CHARACTERISTICS: Mature males distinguished by tusk; all narwhals except calves display black and white mottling; prominent bluff melon and no beak

POPULATION STATUS: Near Threatened (IUCN 2008)

NATURAL PREDATORS: Killer whales, polar bears, and occasionally Greenland sharks and walruses; greatest threat from humans

DIVING ABILITY: Capable of dives of 25 minutes and at 1,500 m

REPRODUCTION: Breeds between late winter and spring, peaking in April; calves born through July and August after 15-month gestation; newborns may nurse for over a year, possibly limiting females to a calving interval of 2-3 years

NARWHAL
Monodon monoceros

The narwhal's most notable asset is the long tusk of adult males. Tusks were sold for extraordinary profits as "unicorn horns" from the Middle Ages until the seventeenth century. As a result, narwhals were known as the "unicorn whale." The male narwhal's tusk is actually a nonfunctional tooth. The upper jaw of all narwhals (males and females) contains two teeth. The teeth never erupt in females. In males, however, the left tooth erupts through the upper lip and spirals outward in a counter-clockwise rotation (from the narwhal's perspective) along a straight core. Exceptions, such as tusked females and males with two tusks, have been seen.

Researchers have always questioned the function of the tusk: theories range from sexual competition between males to spearfishing to drilling through sea ice. In 2005, an interdisciplinary team of researchers discovered the most likely plausible function of this tusk. Embed-

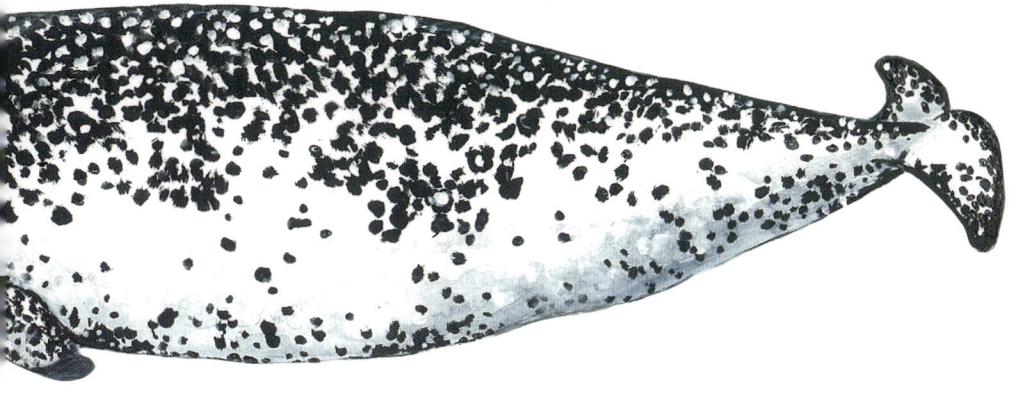

ded in the tusk surface are 10,000 nerve endings possibly capable of determining temperature, pressure (depth), salinity, and other variables. This would allow males to monitor environment conditions, perhaps to select the best breeding and feeding grounds and/or to detect hazardous conditions, such as sea ice freezing around them. The narwhal's tusk is a unique sensory organ in the animal kingdom and may also serve as a secondary sexual characteristic or to display hierarchy among males.

The narwhal is an extreme northern species. Although nearly circumpolar in distribution, more than 85 per cent of its worldwide population occurs in the Canadian high Arctic. The southerly extent of this species is approximately 60° north, or the northerly tip of Labrador, although it has been encountered farther south.

Narwhals are not considered residents of the northwest Atlantic but, rather, extralimital visitors reaching as far south as the island of Newfoundland. These southern narwhals are typically solitary juveniles that may have left or been sepa-

rated from their natal group. These visits are similar, though considerably less frequent, to those of the "friendly" beluga juveniles that occupy a particular harbour for a period of time in Newfoundland and Labrador. This is not healthy or natural behaviour for either species.

Distinguishing characteristics

Quite clearly, the narwhal's most distinctive feature is the tusk on adult males, which can reach lengths up to 3 metres. Both males and females are mottled black and white, with a higher concentration of black spots on the topside and a whiter belly. Calves are all grey, turning black with white speckles as juveniles. As adults

A group of male narwhals at the surface. *Marie Auger-Méthé*

age, they become progressively lighter and even almost entirely white with black remaining only on the face, centreline of the back, and outlines around the fluke and flippers.

The narwhal's head is small and rounded with a prominent melon that may extend forward of the mouth. Narwhals are beakless. The trailing edge of the fluke is convex, similar to that of the beluga. Their pectoral fins are quite short and a dorsal ridge replaces a dorsal fin.

Within the narwhal's range, females and juveniles without an erupted tusk could be confused with the beluga whale. Both belugas and narwhals are gregarious and may be seen in the same area but usually do not form mixed-species groups. Colouration is key: all narwhals have some black on their body; belugas can be white or grey but never black, spotted, or mottled.

Feeding and behaviour

The narwhal's diet is predominantly fish, squid, and shrimp. Arctic fish species— Greenland halibut, Arctic cod, and polar cod—are preferred prey. Deep divers, narwhals take prey from at or near the ocean bottom as well as within the water column.

As the narwhal is one of the most northerly cetacean species, its behaviour is linked to sea ice conditions. The Atlantic portion of this Arctic population annually migrates between two distinct areas. They spend winters offshore in deep waters along the continental slope with a high bottom temperature gradient rate of change; these areas are mostly ice-covered, with predictable areas of open water. After a slow two-month migration, during which time reproduction occurs and peaks in April, they spend summers in ice-free fjords and shallow bays.

The narwhal's behaviour varies greatly between seasons. Recent studies have indicated that, at least among the Atlantic population, intense feeding near the sea floor during the winter contrasts starkly with low levels of foraging during the summer. Not only does the intensity differ between winter and summer grounds but also the diving depth. These seasonal differences suggest that most of the narwhal's annual caloric intake occurs during the winter, and hence the importance of their winter feeding grounds.

Narwhals are gregarious, often observed in groups of hundreds during the summer. These large herds are gatherings of much smaller social groups typically fewer than 20 whales. These smaller groups are relatively homogenous, composed of individuals of the same sex or age class and seen most often on the summering grounds. Individuals are often more scattered and also appear solitary during the winter, possibly because of the patchiness of sea ice, but also likely due to reasons not yet known to scientists.

A young male narwhal photographed in Spaniard's Bay, Newfoundland and Labrador. *DFO*

A pod of narwhals in the northwest Atlantic. Note the length of the males' tusks, which can reach up to 3 metres (9 feet) in length. DFO

Population status

Many surveys have been conducted across a considerable portion of the narwhal's range. Based on these figures and what is known about uncounted populations, the global population estimate is over 80,000, and over 70,000 of the total population summers in the Canadian high Arctic.

Despite these seemingly positive population figures, the narwhal is listed as Near Threatened (2008) because of its high sensitivity to the threats outlined below.

Threats

The narwhal is subject to many direct and indirect threats throughout its geographic range. Intense subsistence hunting in Canada and Greenland (Denmark) remains the longest and most consistent threat. Although only hunted opportunistically by commercial whalers, the narwhal is still, and only, actively hunted in the eastern Canadian Arctic and Greenland, primarily for maktaq (skin and connected blubber) and tusk ivory. A recent rise in the cash value of ivory has dramatically increased the incentive to hunt narwhal.

Although the export of tusks is banned in Greenland, it is allowed in Canada. This ban is supported by catch statistics showing a clear decline in catches in West Greenland since the early 1990s and no evidence of a significant sex bias among those killed. In contrast, most Canadian Arctic communities take a considerably higher proportion of males. Canadian catch statistics are not only incomplete but also likely underestimate the total number of narwhals killed. Although the Canadian hunt is managed, compliance is highly questionable, which compounds the degree of risk narwhals summering in Canadian territory waters face.

Habitat degradation from oil exploration and development, increases in shipping in the high Arctic, and the reduction of sea ice due to climate change are growing threats to narwhals. Because narwhals are not widely distributed, demonstrate high site fidelity, and have specialized habitat requirements, they are considered among the most sensitive of all Arctic marine mammals to climate change and habitat degradation. Continued monitoring and assessment is warranted to understand and protect this species.

TOOTHED SPECIES

ADULT SIZE: 4.6 m (male); 4.4 m (female)

COLOUR: Dark blue-grey topside and light grey belly

SPEED: Unavailable

GROUP SIZE: Thought to occur in groups of 2-7 individuals, or solitary

PRIMARY FOOD: Squid and small fish

DISTINGUISHING CHARACTERISTICS: Males more readily identifiable than many other beaked whale males due to steeply arched lower jawline and two large teeth at its crest, above the top jaw; females do not share these features

POPULATION STATUS: Data Deficient (IUCN 2008)

MORPHOLOGY: Has densest bones of any animal

NAME ORIGIN: Often called "dense-beaked whales" from their species name, which is derived from the Latin *densus* for "thick" or "dense" and *rostrum* for "beak"

BLAINVILLE'S BEAKED WHALE
Mesoplodon densirostris

Blainville's beaked whales are another widely dispersed, cosmopolitan beaked whale that inhabits temperate and tropical waters in all oceans. Their occurrence in higher latitudes is likely associated with warm water currents, such as the Gulf Stream in the North Atlantic. This species likely has the widest distribution of all the species of the *Mesoplodon* genus and are also the most tropical; in most tropical seas, Blainville's beaked whales are considered fairly common.

Blainville's beaked whales may be found throughout the northwest Atlantic as far north as Labrador but are more likely to be found toward the southern and eastern extremes where surface temperatures are much warmer. Like all

Mesoplodons, Blainville's beaked whales are primarily an offshore, deep-water species; it is rarely encountered nearshore except around oceanic islands and other areas where the shoreline connects with deep water. A detailed habitat assessment found that Blainville's beaked whales are commonly encountered in the Bahamas in water depths of 200 to 1,000 metres. A similar assessment in Hawaii found a habitat preference for 700 to 1,000 metres. These habitat preferences likely reflect local underwater topography and prey concentrations in these areas.

Blainville's beaked whales are better studied than similar species because they are relatively easy to identify. In some areas, photo-identification studies of Blainville's beaked whales are being conducted, possibly because of regular at-sea encounters. Ease of identification, however, is limited to adult males; females and young whales are nondescript and often impossible to identify unless they are closely associated with a male in a group.

Distinguishing characteristics

Male Blainville's beaked whales are probably the strangest looking whale in Atlantic Canadian waters. Their body and dorsal fin are shaped much like those of other species in the *Mesoplodon* genus—a robust body at the centre, tapered

Adult male Blainville's beaked whale with barnacles on its erupted teeth.
Robin W. Baird / cascadiaresearch.org

Adult female Blainville's beaked whale seen near Hawaii.
Robin W. Baird / cascadiaresearch.org

evenly to the head and tail, and a small triangular or hooked dorsal fin set back about two-thirds of the way along the body. The colouration, too, is unremarkable, as they are countershaded with a dark grey or blue-grey topside contrasting with a light grey or sometimes light brown-grey belly that extends and blends into the lower jaw and face. Males commonly have long, linear, light-coloured scars; both males and females are often observed with white oval scars, likely from cookie-cutter shark bites.

The feature that allows for relatively easy identification of male Blainville's beaked whales is the shape of the lower jaw: it is steeply arched at its mid-length, rising above the upper jaw in front of the melon and curving slightly downward again toward the eye. At the top of the jawline crest a large triangular-shaped tooth erupts at sexual maturity; it is angled slightly forward and often encrusted with barnacles.

Females have a less pronounced arch in their lower jawline, which does not reach above the top jaw nor does it have an erupted tooth. Their faces are lighter in colour than those of the male and, without prominent and distinct features, they are usually impossible to distinguish at sea.

Blainville's beaked whales can be confused with Cuvier's, True's, and Sowerby's beaked whales in the northwest Atlantic. The male's jawline and teeth are essential to correct identification.

Feeding and behaviour

Similar to other beaked whales, Blainville's beaked whales are deep divers whose primary prey is squid and, sometimes, deep-water fish. As with other species in this genus, Blainville's are likely suction feeders.

Blainville's beaked whales are usually encountered in groups of two to seven individuals or alone. Dives of over 45 minutes have been recorded. Little else is known about this species' biology and behaviour. Even though Blainville's beaked whales may be more observable at sea, much of what is known today is based on stranded specimens and the *Mesoplodon* genus as a whole.

Population status

Blainville's beaked whales are considered Data Deficient by the IUCN. A worldwide population abundance estimate does not exist.

Threats

Blainville's beaked whales are threatened by incidental takes, such as in the Japanese tuna fishery, and by directed takes by hunters. It appears unlikely, however, that either of these takes would occur at a rate that would adversely affect the worldwide population.

The ingestion of plastic is a threat to several beaked whale species, including Blainville's beaked whales. Stomach content analysis of dead stranded whales revealed undigested plastics. Among these individuals, a false sense of being satiated may have caused the whale to stop feeding and subsequently become malnourished and susceptible to disease and death. The extent of this threat is unknown.

The greatest threat to this species is likely impact from loud anthropogenic noises, such as naval sonar and seismic exploration. As with other deep-diving species, mass strandings of Blainville's beaked whales may be correlated with this excessive noise. More research on this subject is warranted.

Adult female and calf Blainville's beaked whales. *Robin W. Baird / cascadiaresearch.org*

TOOTHED SPECIES

ADULT SIZE: 4-5 m; males slightly longer than females

COLOUR: White to off-white to yellowish white

SPEED: Bursts up to 12 knots (22 km/h); typical travelling speed ~1.5-5 knots (3-9 km/h)

GROUP SIZE: 5-20; can congregate in groups of hundreds or thousands

PRIMARY FOOD: Salmon, herring, Arctic cod, and other fish

DISTINGUISHING CHARACTERISTICS: White colouration; dorsal ridge instead of dorsal fin; unfused neck vertebrae allow tilting and turning of head

POPULATION STATUS: Near Threatened (IUCN 2008)

DIVING ABILITY: To 300 m

MORPHOLOGY: Can pucker lips, creating a sucking action while foraging

ACOUSTICS: Called "sea canaries" because of high-pitched vocalizations

BELUGA WHALE
Delphinapterus leucas

The beluga whale, often dubbed the "white whale," is a highly social, gregarious toothed whale that lives only in polar and sub-polar latitudes in the northern hemisphere. Belugas are among the most vocal of all cetaceans, producing sounds ranging from whistles and squeals to clicks and clucks.

Belugas were among the first species to be captured for aquariums and research; they are highly adaptive to new conditions and human training. Their appearance and disposition is unique among whales—belugas can make different expressions by changing the shape of their lips and forehead. Their flexible necks allow them to turn their heads and nod, seeming to express an inquisitive nature.

Belugas were a staple of Arctic communities and hunted for food, oil, and

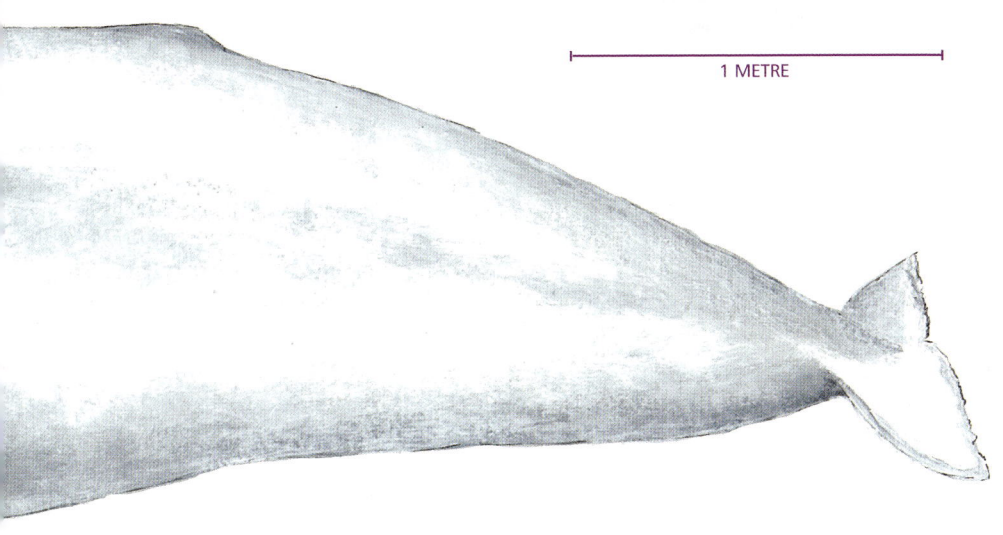

1 METRE

leather. This hunt continues, on a small scale, in 2013. The beluga hunt has also been an important source of information: scientists collect tissue and organ samples from carcasses for research. Radio and satellite tracking have yielded additional data. Belugas are more abundant and have more easily adapted to heavy ice conditions than was previously thought.

Belugas occupy a range of habitats: estuaries, continental shelf, and slope waters; open water, loose ice, and heavy pack ice. Individuals and small groups have been observed entering estuaries and travelling hundreds of kilometres upriver. Belugas spend winters and summers in coastal areas that may be as shallow as 1 to 3 metres, although they do venture offshore. Their winter habitat preference is for areas with light or broken ice conditions. Migration patterns differ among groups and individuals: some migrate thousands of kilometres; others make slight seasonal shifts of several hundred kilometres, usually due to the formation of ice along the coast ("fast ice"). Belugas sometimes move into deep, offshore, ice-covered waters, although this behaviour is not well understood.

Distinguishing characteristics

Adult belugas are uniformly white except for a slight darkening on their dorsal ridge (they do not have a dorsal fin) and on the trailing edges of their flippers and fluke. Newborn belugas are a dark grey-brown, which gradually lightens until adulthood (5-12 years) is reached. As a beluga ages, the trailing edge of its fluke becomes increasingly convex.

An aerial shot of a pod of beluga whales. *Captain Budd Christman / National Oceanic and Atmospheric Administration (NOAA) / Dept. of Commerce*

ATLANTIC CANADA AND NORTHEAST UNITED STATES

Belugas have a short beak and a small head relative to its body size with a rounded melon. Unlike those of other whales and dolphins, the beluga's neck vertebrae are not fused, enabling them to turn, tilt, and nod their heads. Their pliable and expressive mouths can be pursed and puckered.

Belugas are often described as blubbery or pudgy, as they are quite robust and rounded, even showing folds and fat crease marks. Female belugas are considerably smaller than males and have a less pronounced melon. Both sexes have eight to nine pairs of teeth in both upper and lower jaws. The teeth of older individuals can be worn down to the gum line.

Adult belugas are unlikely to be confused with any other species. Because of their darker colouration young and juvenile belugas may be mistaken for narwhals. The narwhal's distinctive blotchy-spotted patterning sets them apart from the beluga; male narwhals often have tusks.

Feeding and behaviour

The diet of belugas varies with location. Salmon, herring, and Arctic cod are their primary prey, although they also feed on squid, octopus, and bottom-dwelling crustaceans such as shrimp and crabs. Belugas feed near or on the sea floor. They are thought to reach depths of over 800 metres and remain submerged for at least 25 minutes.

Belugas sometimes travel into dangerous ice-covered waters. They likely do this to avoid killer whales, but it also increases the risk of ice entrapment, which in turn exposes them to polar bear predation. Scars from polar bear attacks are common within some beluga groups. They may also move to deeper, ice-covered offshore regions for feeding. Because continental shelf breaks tend to be rich in sea life, the large numbers of Arctic cod and other prey in these areas may outweigh the risks of travelling through these ice-covered waters.

Some beluga populations have been shown to maintain strong fidelity to their summering grounds near fjords and estuaries. It is thought that females, in particular, return to the same summering sites their mothers visited.

Belugas often occur in same-sex and same-age class pods. Highly social, groups are often close-knit. Groups of hundreds or thousands of belugas can occur, although they typically consist of 5 to 20 individuals.

Population status

Belugas are listed as Near Threatened by the IUCN. The global population is divided into 29 subpopulations by the IWC. These subpopulations occur over a broad range and are subjected to different threats and levels of risk. As of 2012, the only subpopulation to be assessed is the Cook Inlet (Alaska) population; it qualified for Threatened status. Other stocks, such as many in Arctic Canada and the

A solitary beluga whale in St. Mary's Bay, Newfoundland and Labrador. *Jack Lawson / DFO*

Adult male beluga named Naluark (Inuit for "whitened skin") at Mystic Aquarium in Mystic, Connecticut. Note the small external ear hole behind the eye. This is believed to be non-functional. *Tara S. Stevens*

St. Lawrence River, might be considered Threatened if assessed separately from the global population.

The global population of belugas is estimated at over 150,000, a number that remains uncertain as not all members of their geographic range have been surveyed.

Threats

Belugas are at risk from overexploitation: hunting for human consumption. Beluga populations or groups that return to the same shallow summering grounds each year are especially vulnerable; this likely explains the extinction of some populations.

Contaminants are a major threat.

The small and geographically isolated St. Lawrence River subpopulation is of special concern, as its PCB and chlorinated PCB levels are much higher than those of their Arctic counterparts. A study of these whales has established a link between immune system dysfunction and PCB exposure.

Climate change is also a threat. A consistent reduction in sea ice could lead to a geographic change in distribution, altered reproductive success, and greater exposure to threats such as killer whale predation and human disturbance. Retreating sea ice has caused higher levels of vessel traffic, the expansion of some fisheries, and oil and gas development. These threats will increase as climate changes in the beluga's habitat.

TOOTHED SPECIES

ADULT SIZE: 3.8 m (male); 3.6 m (female)

COLOUR: Dark grey to black with white belly; white scars accumulate on adults to the point they may appear almost white

SPEED: Typical travelling speed ~5 knots (9 km/h)

GROUP SIZE: 12-40; groups of thousands have been observed

PRIMARY FOOD: Cephalopods, specifically squid

DISTINGUISHING CHARACTERISTICS: No prominent beak; relatively large, tall, and erect dorsal fin; extensive scarring across adult bodies

POPULATION STATUS: Least Concern (IUCN 2008)

SURFACE BEHAVIOUR: Young Risso's dolphins breach fully out of the water; adults tend to half-breach; all age classes spyhop, lobtail, and surf waves

HABITAT: Prefer depths >300 m with 10°-28°C surface temperature range

DIVING ABILITY: Up to 30 minutes

RISSO'S DOLPHIN
Grampus griseus

Risso's dolphins are distributed worldwide, typically inhabiting deep, temperate, and tropical offshore waters on the seaward side of the continental shelf edge. It is believed that they prefer certain sea-floor characteristics such as steep bottom topography near deep canyons and gullies.

The Risso's dolphin range in the northwest Atlantic is extensive and, rarely, includes the Gulf of St. Lawrence. The northern limit appears to be southern Labrador. Although the Risso's *range* is large, nearly all sightings are concentrated near the continental slope edge in the southern extremities of this region.

Studies show a strong association

1 METRE

between the Risso's dolphin's habitat preference and the concentration and distribution of squid, their primary food. Oceanographic conditions—such as deep, steep bottom topography, currents, and upwelling—which influence the distribution of squid, are also factors in the Risso's dolphin's occurrence and movement patterns.

Migratory patterns for this species have not been recorded. Since Risso's dolphins appear connected to the movement and presence of their food, a disruption or dramatic alteration of the main prey source could negatively influence local, or possibly more widespread, populations.

Distinguishing characteristics

Risso's dolphins are set apart by a broad, blunt, square, beakless head. The front half of the body is more robust than the tapered trailing half. Adult Risso's dolphins also have unmistakable white patterning due to scarring. The scars are caused mostly by the teeth of other members of the same species and, to a lesser extent, by interactions with squid.

As Risso's dolphins age, scarring may become concentrated on their backs and sides, making them appear almost entirely white, except for their dorsal and pectoral fins.

Risso's dolphins have tall, dark dorsal fins, with curved trailing edges. Their flippers, too, are dark, long, pointed, and sickle shaped.

Colouration beneath the scars ranges from a pale yellow-beige to dark brown to shades of grey. Young calves have a darker grey or brown back, which lightens to cream on their undersides. They are relatively unmarked. Juveniles undergo several colour changes—from pale silver, which darkens to near black, which then lightens as scars are acquired. Risso's dolphins' white lips contrast with the darkened eye area. The adult's ventral surface remains pale grey to white; it features an anchor-shaped chest patch, similar to that of pilot whales, visible when it spyhops and which spreads along the underside to the anus.

Risso's dolphins have two to seven pairs of oval teeth at the front of the bottom jaw. Occasionally, unerupted, vestigial teeth have been found in the top jaw. A feature unique to Risso's dolphins is a crease down the centre of the head, from the blowhole to the upper lip, sometimes dubbed their "cleft melon."

This species is easily identified at sea, especially at close range. At a distance, however, Risso's dolphins may be confused with bottlenose dolphins, pilot whales, and female or juvenile killer whales because of their prominent hooked dorsal fin relative to body size. Because of their light colour, some older adults may be confused with beluga whales.

Feeding and behaviour

Risso's dolphins feed predominantly on squid in deep oceanic and continental slope areas. They also feed on crustaceans, although to a lesser extent. Other types of cephalopods, such as cuttlefish, are seasonal prey in some areas.

Squid tend to remain near the ocean floor during the day and migrate toward the surface at night as a defense against predators. Because of this, Risso's dolphins feed predominantly at night in some areas. Most of their dives are short, only one to two minutes duration with 15- to 20-second breathing intervals between dives. They can also perform up to 30-minute dives.

Risso's dolphins are usually observed in groups of 12 to 40 individuals; the average group size is 25. On some occasions, aggregations numbering several hundreds to thousands have been encountered. These "herds" likely represent a high prey concentration rather than social associations and bonds. Aerial acrobatics and surface behaviour, such as breaching, half-breaching, spyhopping, tail slapping, head-slapping, flipper-slapping, lobtailing, and wave surfing are not uncommon. While they rarely bow-ride, they do occasionally approach vessels and swim in the wake. Risso's dolphins have been observed in mixed-species groups with other toothed whales and dolphins.

Population status

There is no current estimate of Risso's dolphins' global abundance, nor is there knowledge of population trends. Some regional populations have been surveyed and estimates are available for specific regions. A 2006 aerial survey that covered the 2,000-metre depth contour from the southern Gulf of Maine to the upper Bay of Fundy and the entrance of the Gulf of St. Lawrence estimated over 14,000 Risso's dolphins in that region. Over 20,000 individuals are thought to inhabit the waters off the eastern United States.

Long-term and possible permanent changes in distribution and abundance have been observed in some areas. For example, an El Niño event may have influenced a shift in the distribution and relative abundance of Risso's dolphins in the Southern California Bight. There is no information on a worldwide population trend.

Scientists know virtually nothing about the reproductive biology of this species;

A heavily scarred adult Risso's dolphin near Newfoundland and Labrador. *DFO*

This Risso's dolphin, spotted near the Azores islands (Portugal) in the North Atlantic, provides a clear view of the species' blunt, beakless head and massive scarring. *Joao Quaresma / SeaPics.com*

this complicates what is already a poorly understood and documented population status. Given that the species' global distribution is widespread, and appears locally abundant, it is considered Least Concern by the IUCN.

Threats

The Risso's dolphin population faces the same threats as many other dolphins. High and increasing levels of anthropogenic noise, particularly from naval sonar, seismic surveys, and shipping traffic, can disrupt its behaviour and negatively impact local and possibly wider-spread populations. Since Risso's dolphins rely on sound for socializing and feeding, they are likely vulnerable to excessive underwater sounds.

Bycatch in fishing gear poses a constant threat, as does competition with squid fisheries. Some direct and intentional killings of Risso's dolphins have been observed in multi-species fisheries in Sri Lanka, the Caribbean, Indonesia, Japan, Taiwan, and the Philippines. In some regions, especially in Sri Lanka, an estimated 1,000 Risso's dolphins are taken annually from a subpopulation of only 5,500 to 13,000 individuals. This catch rate likely has an adverse effect on the population.

Global climate change may also negatively affect the worldwide population of Risso's dolphins. Since their distribution and density are strongly associated with their prey, which is in turn contingent upon oceanographic conditions, any effect on the prey will be quickly reflected in the dolphin population. The nature of this impact, however, is unclear.

TOOTHED SPECIES

ADULT size: 2-4 m

COLOUR: Dark grey back, lighter grey side, and light grey or pinkish belly

SPEED: Bursts up to 15-19 knots (28-35 km/h); typical travelling speed ~2.5-6 knots (5-11 km/h)

GROUP SIZE: Solitary or fewer than 10

PRIMARY FOOD: Fish and squid

DISTINGUISHING CHARACTERISTICS: Prominent distinction between forehead and beak; large curved dorsal fin located centrally along the back; thick tail stock; among larger dolphins in the northwest Atlantic

POPULATION STATUS: Least Concern (IUCN 2008)

BEHAVIOUR: Highly active at surface, performing acrobatics and breaches, sometimes metres above the water, lobtailing, bow-riding, wake-riding, and wave-surfing; powerful swimmers that outpace some boats

REPRODUCTION: Gestation about 12 months; calves nurse or partially nurse up to 20 months

LIFESPAN: 40-45 (males); at least 50 (females)

COMMON BOTTLENOSE DOLPHIN

Lagenorhynchus albirostris

Common bottlenose dolphins are widely recognized due to their popularity in aquariums and popular media (remember the movie *Flipper*?). When most people hear the word "dolphin," this species comes to mind. Underneath this beloved image, however, the common bottlenose dolphin is complicated, intelligent, and, in the case of some local populations, threatened.

Bottlenose dolphins are the best understood dolphin species, attributed in part to their common nearshore distribution, ability to reproduce successfully in captivity, and long history as aquarium residents. They respond positively to human interaction while in captivity, allowing researchers to test hypotheses and collect data that would be impossible with any marine mammal in its natural habitat.

1 METRE

There is a caveat: as the subject specimens were in captivity and not in their natural environment, they might behave or biologically function differently than if they were in the ocean.

Common bottlenose dolphins are found throughout the world in temperate, subtropical, and tropical waters and inshore, coastal, shelf, and oceanic waters. They do occur in the northwest Atlantic, although rarely reaching the higher latitudes of Newfoundland and Labrador. In some places in eastern Canada (and throughout the world), bottlenose dolphins can be seen from the shoreline and beaches.

Because of taxonomic, morphological, behavioural, and ecological variances, different subspecies of bottlenose dolphins have been suggested. For example, in many areas throughout the world, including the northwest Atlantic, two varieties exist: a coastal bottlenose dolphin and an offshore bottlenose dolphin. These are more easily distinguished (based on morphology, genetics, and habitat) in the North Atlantic and may be classified as separate species.

Distinguishing characteristics

Bottlenose dolphins are generally easily identified by their shape and colour. At a distance, however, confusion between most dolphin species is possible. In the northwest Atlantic, the bottlenose

An acrobatic common bottlenose dolphin. *Adam Li / NOAA / Dept. of Commerce*

Mother and juvenile bottlenose dolphins head toward the sea floor.
M. Herko / OAR / National Undersea Research Program / NOAA

dolphin would likely be mistaken for Risso's dolphin because of its larger size and colouration.

Bottlenose dolphins vary considerably in size, shape, and colour. In general, they are large and robust with a prominent beak and a sharp crease between melon and beak. When they are viewed from a distance, bottlenose dolphins appear uniform in colour, ranging from light grey to blue-grey to nearly black. Upon closer inspection, it is clear that they have a darker "cape" along the top portion of the back, paler sides, and an off-white or greyish underside. Some spotting along the sides might be evident, especially in older adults.

The bottlenose dolphin's dark dorsal fin is located in the centre of its back. It is prominent and slightly curved or hooked. Offshore dolphins tend to be larger and broader than their inshore counterparts.

Feeding and behaviour

Bottlenose dolphins consume a wide variety of prey. Fish and squid are their main diet, although they have been known to prey on shrimp and other crustaceans. They are opportunistic feeders, taking advantage of the most abundant suitable prey in an area. Bottlenose dolphins may feed cooperatively, such as on schooling fish, or separately, and have been known to follow shrimp trawlers.

As with most dolphin species, bottlenose dolphins are social and live in groups, although group composition can change daily. Groups usual have fewer than 20 individuals, although groups of over 100 have been documented in offshore regions. Coastal bottlenose dolphins maintain long-term, multi-generational home ranges, while offshore dolphins appear less restricted in their range and movement patterns. Some offshore populations have shown site fidelity around oceanic islands, however, and some nearshore populations are migratory. The density of the coastal variety is higher than that of the oceanic type.

Bottlenose dolphins are often seen in association with large whales as well as mixed-species dolphin groups. They are quite active at the surface, and tail-slapping and various forms of acrobatic breaches are observed regularly. Higher activity rates are often associated with feeding and socializing events.

Population status

Bottlenose dolphins are currently listed as Least Concern by the IUCN. The species is widespread and abundant. Although there are local threats for certain populations, none are thought likely to cause a major global population decline. A minimum worldwide estimate for bottlenose dolphins is approximately 600,000

There is a prominent distinction between a bottlenose dolphin's head and beak—a distinguishing feature of this species. *Wayne Hoggard / NOAA / Dept. of Commerce*

individuals. The current population trend is not available.

Threats

Incidental fisheries catches and directed kills or other forms of exploitation likely pose the greatest threat to the global bottlenose dolphin population. Typically, nearshore and island-associated populations are at a higher risk as they are in closer and more frequent contact with humans.

Bottlenose dolphins can become accidentally caught in fisheries that use gill-nets, drift nets, purse seines, trawls, longlines, and hook and line gear. Mortality rates due to incidental catches are often poorly documented and may increase as humans expand their fishing activities.

Directed catches, such as harpooning individuals, or groups that are driven to shore and killed, are an even greater threat than those posed by fishing activities. They are targeted not only to reduce competition with commercial and small-scale fishing activities but also for bait, food, and commercial products. This has been reported worldwide, but mortality rates are highest in the Mediterranean and Black seas, Sri Lanka, Peru, Taiwan, Japan, and the Faroe Islands. Live captures of bottlenose dolphins for aquariums, research, and military applications (such as training for underwater bomb detection) continues throughout the species' range and has had a negative effect on populations in the Gulf of Mexico and the southeastern United States.

Other risks include exposure to toxic chemicals, which might affect the dolphin's reproductive success and immune system, and habitat degradation, which includes acoustic disturbances, interaction with boats and vessels, and competition for prey.

TOOTHED SPECIES

ADULT SIZE: 3 m (male); 2.8 m (female)

COLOUR: Complex colouration pattern of black to grey to white

Speed: High-speed swimmers capable of speeds >20 knots (37 km/h); a distinctive "rooster-tail" while porpoising

GROUP SIZE: Solitary or 5-50 individuals

PRIMARY FOOD: Small pelagic schooling fish such as capelin and herring

DISTINGUISHING CHARACTERISTICS: Complex grey-white-black colouration with distinctive grey-white tail stock, contrasting sharply with dark dorsal fin area; robust with short, thick beak and large, tall, and curved dorsal fin

POPULATION STATUS: Least Concern (IUCN 2008)

ACOUSTICS: Highly vocal, producing whistles in 3-35 kHz range

ASSOCIATIONS: With large whales, such as fin and humpback; mixes with other dolphin species such as white-sided dolphins

CALVING: Little is known about their reproduction biology; calving likely occurs May to September

WHITE-BEAKED DOLPHIN
Lagenorhynchus albirostris

White-beaked dolphins, found only in the North Atlantic Ocean, are relatively common in the northwest Atlantic. They inhabit cold, temperate, and sub-polar waters on both sides of the Atlantic Ocean and are widespread and abundant throughout this range. Research indicates a possible habitat preference for waters less than 200 metres deep; they inhabit inshore, continental shelf, and offshore waters and prefer the shelf edge. This habitat use is likely related to their prey and feeding behaviour; however, few studies have focused on white-beaked dolphins.

The white-beaked dolphin's name is derived from its white beak, although not all individuals actually have white beaks. While this species has been given countless nicknames, "squid-hounds" (due to

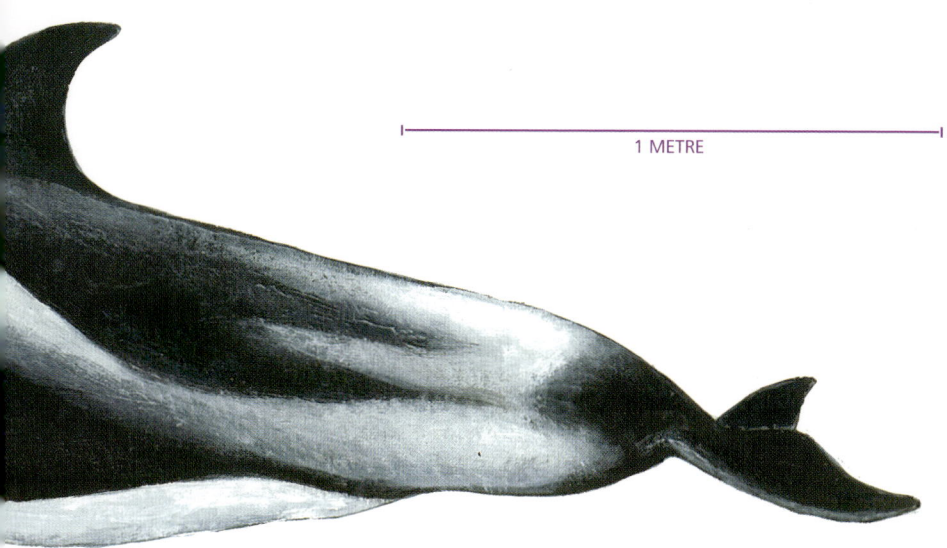

1 METRE

their preference for squid) and "jumpers" (for their acrobatic surface behaviour) are common among fishers in Atlantic Canada.

Distinguishing characteristics

White-beaked dolphins are among the largest oceanic dolphins in the northwest Atlantic. In fact, their size and shape are key identifying characteristics. They have a large, tall, and hooked dorsal fin, which is more prominent in adult males. Their beaks are short, thick, and variable in colour, although they are most commonly white.

The colour and pattern of the rest of the body is variable. The dorsal fin and upper side is mostly dark grey, although often interrupted by a white or light grey swath behind the dorsal fin that diffuses downward across its thick tail stock. This lighter colouration usually connects to an even lighter and more variable blaze that extends to its face. The white-beaked dolphin's underside is white, which reaches to the tail stock. This usually contrasts sharply with a dark flank below the lighter blaze pattern. The dolphin's pectoral fins and flukes have pointed tips and are usually dark grey or black.

A relatively large dorsal fin is key to distinguishing the white-beaked dolphin.
Nadine and Thierry Vogenstahl

Studies have revealed a morphological difference between white-beaked dolphins in eastern and western Atlantic. It has been suggested in scientific literature that the observable characteristics of the east and west populations have evolved from the species' interaction with its environment or habitat. Although this warrants further research, it does indicate that eastern and western groups do not mix.

White-beaked dolphins are powerful and fast swimmers. When they surface at quick speeds, their dorsal fins create a splash of water that rises above the fin in a V-shape—called a "rooster-tail," a characteristic of this species in the northwest Atlantic. White-beaked dolphins can often be identified at a distance because of their swim pattern and rooster-tails.

White-beaked dolphins may be confused with the Atlantic white-sided dolphin and the short-beaked common dolphin. However, the white-beak's robust size and lack of a yellow streak (characteristic of the other two species) is likely adequate for correct identification, especially at close range. At first sight, they may be confused with female or juvenile killer whales because of their similar dorsal fin colour and shape. The distinct black and white pattern and larger body size of killer whales set them apart.

Feeding and behaviour

White-beaked dolphins feed on a variety of prey, predominantly small pelagic schooling fish such as capelin and herring. Benthic fish (such as cod and haddock), crustaceans, and squid are also consumed by this species. In addition to feeding alone deep underwater, white-beaked dolphins feed cooperatively and corral schooling fish near the ocean surface.

White-beaked dolphins associate with baleen whales, such as fin and humpback whales, while they are feeding, acting as scavengers as the large whale approaches the surface with a mouthful of fish. White-beaks will readily join the surfacing whale to eat the prey that comes out of its mouth. They may also follow these whales as they move with their prey but likely do not coordinate efforts with other whales.

White-beaked dolphins do, however, form mixed-species groups with other dolphins such as bottlenose and Atlantic white-sided dolphins. This, too, is most likely linked to a common prey.

Acoustics play a strong role in the ecology and behaviour of white-beaked dolphins. While they are highly vocal, little research has been devoted to learning about their acoustic repertoire and its significance and usage. White-beaks produce whistles in the 3-35 kHz range, likely for orientation and possible communication, in addition to echolocation during feeding. It is not known if this species produces tonal, or pulsed, vocalizations as other dolphins do.

White-beaked dolphins are gregarious and are often found in groups of 5 to 50

White-beaked dolphins are gregarious and acrobatic. Note the characteristic white streak along its side and flank.
Nadine and Thierry Vogenstahl

A white-beaked dolphin leaping out of the water near St-Pierre-et-Miquelon.
Nadine and Thierry Vogenstahl

individuals. Groups numbering several hundreds have been reported. This suggests a segregation of age groups; juveniles may separate from groups composed of adults and calves, forming their own schools.

White-beaked dolphins of any age class often display acrobatics above the surface. They frequently approach boats from a distance to bow-ride and jump in the vessel's wake.

Population status

Few abundance estimates exist for this species, although some suggest there are 100,000 or more, with 10,000 white-beaked dolphins in the northwest Atlantic. In Newfoundland and Labrador, white-beaked dolphins are likely the most common dolphin species encountered at sea. While their numbers do not appear to be declining, the population trend, whether stable or increasing, remains unknown.

Given their widespread distribution, high abundance levels, and no reports of population decline, white-beaked dolphins are classified as Least Concern by the IUCN.

Threats

White-beaked dolphins are subject to common threats, including noise disturbances, incidental entrapments in fishing gear as bycatch, and contamination by organochlorines, heavy metals, and other pollutants that may disrupt their reproduction.

Since white-beaked dolphins are found in colder North Atlantic waters, ice entrapments do occur, but pose a minor risk to individuals and groups. These dolphins have been the target of small-scale hunting throughout their range, including off Greenland and Labrador. It is believed that, although this species is subject to potential threats, mortality rates are not high enough to pose a serious threat. While little is known about white-beaked dolphins' reproduction, their birth rate balances or exceeds their mortality rate.

TOOTHED SPECIES

ADULT SIZE: 2.8 m (male); 2.4 m (female)

COLOUR: Complex colouration: black topside, grey side and lower tail stock, white underside; yellowish patch above a white patch behind dorsal fin; black flippers, dorsal fin, and fluke

SPEED: Travels long distances maintaining 7 knots (13 km/h); may reach speeds of 25 knots (46 km/h)

GROUP SIZE: Average 5-15 individuals; gatherings of several hundred to socialize, migrate, or feed

PRIMARY FOOD: Small schooling fish, such as herring, mackerel, smelt, and sand lance, as well as shrimp, squid, and some bottom-dwelling fish

DISTINGUISHING CHARACTERISTICS: Yellowish patch on flank; black ring around eye; relatively unpronounced beak, black on top, white underneath; features usually visible during surfacing or acrobatics

POPULATION STATUS: Least Concern (IUCN 2008)

DISTRIBUTION: Limited to temperate and cold-temperate North Atlantic

POPULATION SIZE: Recent estimates indicate ~51,000 in Atlantic Canada and northern US seaboard; estimated 12,000 summer in Gulf of St. Lawrence

ASSOCIATIONS: Commonly with humpback and fin whales in the northwest Atlantic; in groups with other dolphin species, primarily white- and short-beaked common dolphins

ATLANTIC WHITE-SIDED DOLPHIN
Lagenorhynchus acutus

The Atlantic white-sided dolphin is a uniquely coloured cetacean found in the cold temperate and sub-polar waters of the North Atlantic. Often referred to as "white-sides" by researchers, they also carry the name "jumpers," given by eastern Canadian fishers because of their acrobatic behaviour.

White-sided dolphins are abundant throughout their range. They inhabit nearshore, continental shelf, and continental slope waters, as well as deep oceanic waters across the North Atlantic. They have also been found relatively far up the St. Lawrence River. Along the continental slope, Atlantic white-sided dolphins prefer habitat with high ocean floor relief and along the shelf edge, likely

1 METRE

due to prey abundance.

In the northwest Atlantic, some white-sided dolphins undergo a seasonal migration, albeit on a significantly smaller scale than that of mysticetes. For example, an abundance of white-sided dolphins in 2013 is observed at the southern limit of their range during the winter and spring. This concentration moves to higher latitudes for the summer and fall. At the same time, many white-sided dolphins move east-west to follow their prey. They are generally seen closer to shore in summer and farther offshore in winter.

Distinguishing characteristics

The Atlantic white-sided dolphin is robust and streamlined, with a short, thick beak and an unpronounced melon. The species name *acutus* translates from Latin

A pair of Atlantic white-sided dolphins surface amidst shipping traffic near St-Pierre-et-Miquelon. *Nadine and Thierry Vogenstahl*

as "sharp" or "pointed," in reference to its dorsal fin, although the flippers and fluke tips are also pointed. While the dorsal fin of adult males is larger and less curved than that of adult females, all white-sided dolphins display a tall and hooked dorsal fin.

The most striking attribute of Atlantic white-sided dolphins is the clearly defined patterning and unusual colour. This species is only one of two whale or dolphin species worldwide that has a conspicuous and pigmented marking in a shade other than black, grey, or white. All Atlantic white-sided dolphins have a wide and elongated yellow to yellow-tan streak on both sides of the upper tail stock.

The short-beaked common dolphin, too, has a yellow patch on its body, but it is less clearly demarcated and vivid than that of the Atlantic white-sided dolphin. The Pacific white-sided dolphin (considered a different species and not described in this book) does not have a yellowish band.

The rest of the Atlantic white-sided dolphin's body is countershaded—darker on top and lighter belly—although not diffusely like that of most other cetaceans. The white-sided dolphin's back, dorsal fin, flippers, and fluke are black or dark grey. Its yellowish patch is mostly encapsulated by the black, but also borders a long white patch, which is nearly centred, on its side. A light grey stripe extends from the posterior of the beak to the fluke, and the underside from the front of the tail stock to the beak is white. Its eyes are circled by a dark patch, creating the illusion of larger, circular eyes. The borders of each colour patch or shaded area are clearly defined.

Among similar species that overlap in distribution with the Atlantic white-sided dolphin in eastern Canada, the most likely to be confused are the short-beaked common dolphin and the white-beaked dolphin. The presence and location of the yellow patch, which is at the front on the short-beaked common dolphin and near the tail on the white-sided dolphin (and absent on the white-beaked dolphin), is usually sufficient to make a positive species identification.

Feeding and behaviour

Atlantic white-sided dolphins feed predominantly on small schooling fish such as herring, mackerel, smelt, and sand lance as well as on shrimp, squid, and some benthic fish.

They have been observed feeding cooperatively with group members. They often associate with large feeding mysticetes, such as humpback and fin whales, as well as with other dolphin species to form mixed groups.

Like most other oceanic dolphin species, Atlantic white-sided dolphins are fast swimmers and commonly perform acrobatics above the surface. Although they do bow- and wake-ride, they appear more wary of vessels than other dolphin species found in the northwest Atlantic. Atlantic white-sided dolphins live in groups of 5-15 individuals; group stability and the strength of social bonds among group members is poorly understood, although there is a degree of social bonding among individuals. Similar to several other species, juvenile white-sided dolphins seem to separate from their adult groups for a time. Gatherings number hundreds or more for foraging, socializing, or migrating.

Population status

Atlantic white-sided dolphins are listed as Least Concern by the IUCN. They are

The light forward patch and crisp stripes of the Atlantic white-sided dolphin help distinguish it from other species. *Nadine and Thierry Vogenstahl*

abundant throughout their entire range, with an estimated 51,000 individuals or more in Atlantic Canada and the northern United States seaboard; across the North Atlantic, the species' population likely exceeds 100,000 individuals. Nearly 12,000 summer in the Gulf of St. Lawrence alone.

Although there is no evidence of a marked population decline in Atlantic white-sided dolphins, it is also not known if it is increasing.

Threats

The threats identified for this species are not sufficiently severe to cause population decline, but they are varied and common among other dolphin species. These disturbances include increasing anthropogenic noise, fishing gear bycatch, and organochlorine, heavy metal, and other pollutant contamination.

Directed hunts for Atlantic white-sided dolphins are ongoing in 2013 in Greenland, the Faroe Islands, and eastern Canada. These hunts are not regulated, but they will not cause a major population decline.

Perhaps the most serious threat to Atlantic white-sided dolphins is as bycatch in midwater trawl nets, specifically mackerel nets. Several studies found that Atlantic white-sided dolphins are the most common dolphin species to be caught in pelagic trawls and that all bycatches were at night. They have been frequently observed feeding near nets during tows, increasing the risk of incidental capture. Studies using underwater photography and video focused within trawl nets show dolphins swimming *inside* of the nets, not only grabbing fish but also wake-riding and appearing to play. Clearly, this behaviour is risky and scientists are looking for ways to deter these dolphins from entering nets.

TOOTHED SPECIES

ADULT SIZE: 2.7 m (male); 2.6 m (female)

COLOUR: Dark grey to black back; light grey tail stock; yellowish patch both sides forward of dorsal fin; white belly

SPEED: Up to 21 knots (39 km/h); typical travelling speed ~5 knots (9 km/h)

GROUP SIZE: Often groups of several hundred individuals

PRIMARY FOOD: Squid and schooling fish

DISTINGUISHING CHARACTERISTICS: Grey and yellow "hourglass" colouration on the side; distinct beak and prominent dorsal fin

POPULATION STATUS: Least Concern (IUCN 2008)

BEHAVIOUR: Highly active at surface, often jump and splash repeatedly; group gathering can exceed thousands of individuals; often highly energetic at the surface, coordinate swimming and surfacing patterns, and enthusiastically bow-ride

ACOUSTICS: Highly vocal, producing whistles, tonal calls, and echolocation; calls or chirps (7-15 kHz) are heard above the surface when alongside a boat

REPRODUCTION: Calving in northern latitudes peaks in late spring and early summer; gestation 10-11 months; healthy females can have one calf every two years under optimal conditions

SHORT-BEAKED COMMON DOLPHIN
Delphinus delphis

The common dolphin is found worldwide; it is abundant in the Pacific and Atlantic oceans and several enclosed seas, especially the Mediterranean Sea and the Sea of Japan. There are two forms of common dolphins: short- and long-beaked. Recently, they were placed in separate species due to morphologic and genetic dissimilarities. Only the short-beaked common dolphin is present in Canada or the northeast United States.

Classified as an ocean rather than a river dolphin, the short-beaked common dolphin is distributed from warm tropical to cool temperate waters worldwide. Their habitat range includes nearshore areas and deep offshore waters thousands of kilometres from land.

1 METRE

Short-beaked common dolphins prefer a habitat with sharp sea-floor relief that creates upwelling to bring concentrations of nutrients and, therefore, potential prey toward the surface. Such areas are prevalent along the continental shelf break. These dolphins are widespread along the continental shelf and can be closely associated with particular oceanographic conditions such as high salinity, shallow thermoclines, warm water currents, and/or shallow, warm, upper surface layers.

In the northwest Atlantic, common dolphins are abundant in the southern Gulf of Maine, where complex bottom topography and the interaction of the warm Gulf Stream with the cold Labrador Current create strong upwelling conditions.

An acrobatic pod of short-beaked common dolphins near St-Pierre-et-Miquelon.
Nadine and Thierry Vogenstahl

Distinguishing characteristics

Of the whale and dolphin species, only the short-beaked common dolphin and the white-sided dolphin have pigmentation other than shades of black, grey, and white. The common dolphin's colour pattern allows easy at-sea identification: a broad, horizontal, yellow to yellowish tan patch on both sides of its front half, called the thoracic patch, contrasts sharply with its dark back and white belly. The tail stock is light grey and joins the tail end of the thoracic patch, creating a criss-cross that resembles an hourglass. Although variable in shape, this hourglass pattern is unique to short-beaked common dolphins.

Dolphins are usually first distinguished by their dorsal fin, which varies from nearly triangular to sickle shaped, with varying degrees of concavity of the trailing edge. The fins are large, dark, and, by adulthood, display a grey centre.

The pectoral fins and fluke are dark grey to black on both sides. Similar to white-sided dolphins, short-beaked common dolphins have a dark circle around each eye, although the leading edge streaks forward above the beak in the latter. Contrary to their name, short-beaked common dolphins have a prominent, large, usually dark beak. There is a distinct crease between forehead and beak.

In the northwest Atlantic, short-beaked common dolphins may be confused with white-sided dolphins and, to a lesser extent, striped dolphins. Short-beaked common dolphins have a more slender, streamlined body than white-sided dolphins as well as a longer beak. The hourglass pattern and location of the yellowish tan thoracic patch is usually enough to distinguish short-beaked common dolphins from other species.

Short-beaked common dolphins swimming alongside the photographer's boat. Note the distinct hourglass pattern on its side. *Kristin O'Brien / Whitehead Lab, Dalhousie University*

Feeding and behaviour

The prey of choice for short-beaked common dolphins is squid and small schooling fish such as mackerel, herring, and smelt. Short-beaked common dolphins' movements and distribution are sometimes associated with a particular prey.

The distinctive yellow-tan patch is visible on the dolphin's side.
Nadine and Thierry Vogenstahl

Short-beaked common dolphins are gregarious and are most frequently observed in schools of hundreds or even

Short-beaked common dolphins often perform acrobatic displays above the water's surface. *Nadine and Thierry Vogenstahl*

thousands. Usually, however, these large schools are composed of smaller groups of 30 or fewer that gather over a large area. These dolphins frequently associate with other whales and dolphins, such as striped and Risso's dolphins, to form mixed-species groups, typically at a productive feeding location.

Short-beaked common dolphins are often active at the surface, porpoising, jumping, splashing, and performing acrobatics, including mid-air somersaults. They are fast swimmers, and expert bow riders at high speeds. Short-beaked common dolphins, like others in the dolphin family (Delphinidae), are highly vocal and can be heard above the surface.

A surfacing common dolphin, with the island of St-Pierre in the background. *Nadine and Thierry Vogenstahl*

TOOTHED SPECIES

DWARF SPERM WHALE

ADULT SIZE: 2.4 m

COLOUR: Blue-grey to dark grey-black back with paler, sometimes pinkish, underside

SPEED: Unavailable

GROUP SIZE: 1-2, possibly up to 10

PRIMARY FOOD: Cephalopods

DISTINGUISHING CHARACTERISTICS: Square-shaped head; false gill; small and underslung jaw; short and robust body; prominent, pointed dorsal fin

POPULATION STATUS: Data Deficient (IUCN 2008)

PYGMY SPERM WHALE

ADULT SIZE: 3 m

COLOUR: Blue-grey to steel grey back and paler, sometimes pink, underside

SPEED: Unavailable

GROUP SIZE: 3-6

PRIMARY FOOD: Cephalopods

DISTINGUISHING CHARACTERISTICS: False gill, small and underslung jaw, and robust body like dwarf sperm whale, but slightly larger, with slightly less squarish head and much smaller and hooked dorsal fin

DWARF SPERM WHALE
Kogia sima

and

PYGMY SPERM WHALE
Kogia breviceps

Dwarf and pygmy sperm whales (family Kogiidae) and sperm whale (family Physeteridae) are named for the spermaceti organ in their head. Spermaceti is similar to a liquid wax, but the organ's function remains uncertain. Dwarf and pygmy sperm whales have a similar appearance. Inconspicuous and rarely observed, and thought to occur mainly offshore, they are among the least understood whales and dolphins worldwide.

Dwarf sperm whale.

1 METRE

Considered a single species until 1966, dwarf and pygmy sperm whales are still confused with one another. They are misidentified as sharks initially at most strandings because of their false gill, small, underslung jaw, and sharp teeth. At sea and even at close range, it may still be impossible to distinguish between these species.

Due to their inconspicuous nature and the difficulty in distinguishing between them, the range and habitat of dwarf and pygmy sperm whales are not certain. Based on rare sightings, stranded individuals, and stomach content analysis, pygmy sperm whales tend to inhabit offshore areas, seaward of the continental slope, and are distributed slightly farther north; dwarf sperm whales may prefer slope-edge waters and warmer habitats. Some researchers consider the Bay of Fundy to be the northern extent of the dwarf sperm whale, while pygmy sperm whales may occur farther north, perhaps to the Strait of Belle Isle between Newfoundland and southern Labrador.

Distinguishing characteristics

Dwarf and pygmy sperm whales feature a single false gill on either side of the head, behind the eye. Both species have a squarish head, small, underslung lower jaw, and short, broad flippers.

Their robust bodies are relatively short, with a blue-grey to dark grey back and a paler, sometimes pinkish underside. The only significant difference between them is that dwarf sperm whales are slightly shorter (by less than 50 centimetres), have a slightly more squarish head, and have a larger and sometimes more curved dorsal fin. Although impossible to view at sea, dwarf sperm whales also have fewer teeth than pygmy sperm whales.

The dwarf sperm whale is the smallest

of all whale species and is even smaller than some dolphins. Either species may be confused with some dolphin species, although the square head and a false gill generally set them apart.

Feeding and behaviour

Deep-water cephalopods (octopus, squid, etc.) are the primary prey of both dwarf and pygmy sperm whales, although they also eat other prey, such as deep-sea fish and shrimp. Some foraging is thought to occur at or near the ocean bottom in deep areas. Very little is known about their feeding behaviour; most of what researchers know is based on stomach content analysis and what is known about the habitat and behaviour of the prey found there.

A rare photograph of pygmy sperm whales, seen in the Pacific Ocean near Indonesia. Note the whales' pinkish undersides. *David B. Fleetham / SeaPics.com*

Pygmy sperm whale.

|—————————————— 1 METRE ——————————————|

Unlike other small whales and dolphins, dwarf and pygmy sperm whales surface slowly and steadily, without a rolling motion, and simply sink away after taking a breath. Both species have been observed while breaching and neither is likely to approach boats. Both can lie motionless at the ocean's surface and are reportedly startled when a boat approaches, subsequently expelling a red-brown cloud of intestinal fluid before diving away. This may be an evolutionary tactic to frighten and confuse potential prey.

Population status

There is no confident worldwide population estimate for either of these species, and their population trend remains unknown. One survey estimates 400 dwarf and pygmy sperm whales combined in western North Atlantic waters. An estimate for Atlantic Canadian waters does not exist. Both species are listed by the IUCN as Data Deficient.

Threats

Threats to dwarf and pygmy sperm whales are poorly understood. Although they were never a target species during the whaling era, both species may have been occasionally harpooned during the nineteenth century. It is believed that small takes of both species still occur in this century in Japan, Indonesia, Taiwan, the Lesser Antilles, and Sri Lanka. Few are thought to die from interactions with fishing boats or equipment or, separately, as bycatch.

The extent to which anthropogenic sound negatively affects these two species is unknown. Loud sounds harm some deep-diving whale species and, since both dwarf and pygmy sperm whales are deep divers, they may be more vulnerable than previously estimated. More research is needed to understand the possible threats to these two rarely seen species.

TOOTHED SPECIES

ADULT SIZE: 2.4 m (male); 2.4 m (female)

COLOUR: Dark back and dorsal fin; light grey blaze, side, and flank; white belly; distinctive black stripe separates light grey side and flank from white underside

SPEED: Typical travelling speeds 15-17 knots (28-31 km/h); can reach 20 knots (37 km/h) or more

GROUP SIZE: Gregarious; often in groups of 100 or more, possibly 500

PRIMARY FOOD: Varied diet: small schooling fish and squid to benthopelagic cod and lantern fish

DISTINGUISHING CHARACTERISTICS: Black stripe from eye along upper part of belly to tail stock; white belly and light grey side and flank; dark, prominent beak and dorsal fin

POPULATION STATUS: Least Concern (IUCN 2008)

DIVING ABILITY: Can last 5-10 minutes; feed mostly near ocean floor at 200-700 m

REPRODUCTION: Female gestation period 12 months or slightly longer; typically calve in late summer to fall; calving interval about 4 years; females sexually immature until age 12

LIFESPAN: 58 years

STRIPED DOLPHIN
Stenella coeruleoalba

The striped dolphin's scientific name *Stenella coeruleoalba*, which refers to its colouration and patterning, is derived from the Latin *caeruleus* and *albus* for "sky blue" and "white." A distinctive stripe beneath its dorsal fin prompted its common name.

A cosmopolitan species, striped dolphins are found in the Pacific, Atlantic, and Indian oceans and other seas. Found abundantly in warm tropical to subtropical waters, striped dolphins also occur in warm temperate latitudes. In the northwest Atlantic, the northern extent of the striped dolphin's distribution is Newfoundland, where its presence is associated with the warm Gulf Stream surface current. Its distribution in these waters shows a preference for highly productive

1 METRE

areas along deep continental slope waters, corresponding to the general route of the Gulf Stream. Since striped dolphin are less common on the landward side of the continental slope margin, near-shore sightings in the northwest Atlantic are less frequent than for other dolphin species.

Distinguishing characteristics

As their name suggests, striped dolphins are distinguished by their stripes: a light grey stripe, or blaze, runs from just in front of its eye at an upward angle to the anterior base of its dorsal fin.

Below the stripe, a light grey colour travels the length of its body and diffuses

A pod of striped dolphins near the Azores islands (Portugal) in the North Atlantic Ocean. *Doug Perrine / SeaPics.com*

along the tail stock. The pattern and colour vary. Their topside and dorsal fins are dark grey to dark grey-blue. This, with the white belly outlined by a long black stripe, contrasts with the lighter grey and creates a visible stripe.

The bodies of striped dolphins are moderately robust and long with tall and strongly curved dorsal fins. These dolphins have a dark, prominent beak and lighter and relatively small pectoral fins and fluke.

In the northwest Atlantic, the only species likely to be confused with the striped dolphin is the short-beaked common dolphin; this is due to their similar slender form, overlap in distribution, and similar schooling patterns (both occur in relatively large social or feeding groups). Attention to the colouration, however, will eliminate confusion: the short-beaked common dolphin's hourglass patterning is different than the thin dark line that extends from the striped dolphin's eye to its tail stock.

Feeding and behaviour

The diet of striped dolphins is as varied as its distribution. Although little data exists for the diet of striped dolphins in the northwest Atlantic, those outside this area consume small schooling fish, squid, and benthopelagic cod and lantern fish. In most areas, striped dolphins appear to feed mostly at depths of 200-700 metres.

Striped dolphins are gregarious and typically occur in groups of 100, or even 500. They are active at the surface, even while travelling, by churning the ocean's surface with their fast porpoising or leaping-style swimming.

Population status

The worldwide striped dolphin population is estimated to be over 2 million, although the trend is unknown. The IUCN lists them as a species of Least Concern. In the western North Atlantic, there are an estimated 92,000 striped dolphins. No population estimate exists for the northwest Atlantic.

Striped dolphins are fast swimmers and can leap up to 7 metres (20 feet) out of the water. *Joao Quaresma / SeaPics.com*

The dolphin's namesake stripes are clearly visible under the water.
Wayne Hoggard / NOAA / Dept. of Commerce

Threats

As with similar species, the striped dolphin faces threats. Although a combination of these threats is unlikely to cause a major global population decline, the possible effects on smaller or isolated subpopulations is unclear.

The leading worldwide threat to striped dolphins is incidental bycatch in fishing gear, namely pelagic drift nets, gill-nets, and purse seines. The use of high seas drift gill-nets during the 1970s and 1980s, mostly in the central and western North Pacific and Mediterranean Sea, likely killed tens of thousands of striped dolphins. Even though some of these fishing practices have been banned, that rate of incidental mortality is not considered sufficient to cause a major population decline. Still, mortality due to fishing operations remains high worldwide. A secondary effect of fishing, such as that of reduced availability of prey, may be an increasing threat as fishery operations expand.

Striped dolphins are threatened by the same risks as other whales and dolphins. For example, high contaminant levels, including organochlorine pollutants such as DDT and PCB, likely cause reproductive impairment and immunosuppressive effects. Not only would this impact their reproductive cycle but it also makes striped dolphins more vulnerable to infection. From 1990 to 1992, several thousand striped dolphins in the Mediterranean Sea died, primarily due to a widespread morbillivirus infection. There, striped dolphins are contaminated with heavy metals and organochlorines. In other areas of the world, however, little is known about contaminant levels in local subpopulations. Further research and protective measures are warranted.

TOOTHED SPECIES

ADULT SIZE: 1.5 m (male); 1.6 m (female)

COLOUR: Dark grey to black back with lighter grey sides blending toward a white belly

SPEED: Average 1-8 knots (2-15 km/h); capable of quicker sprints

GROUP SIZE: Typically solitary and nonsocial; can occur in groups of 2-5 individuals

PRIMARY FOOD: Fish and cephalopods, vary across their range; schooling fish, such as herring and capelin, are prey of choice in northwest Atlantic

DISTINGUISHING CHARACTERISTICS: Only porpoise species and smallest cetacean in Atlantic Canada; identifiable by triangular dorsal fin and quick, rolling surfacing movement pattern

POPULATION STATUS: Least Concern (IUCN 2008)

MOVEMENTS: Highly mobile; home range of thousands of square kilometres; often travel tens of kilometres per day

LIFESPAN: Mature between 2 and 4 years, rarely live longer than 20 years

DIVING ABILITY: Less than 90 seconds, but dives up to 5 minutes recorded; dive depth 20-130 m; dives to >200 m occur

HARBOUR PORPOISE
Phocoena phocoena

The harbour porpoise is the smallest cetacean in Atlantic Canadian waters. Although the harbour porpoise is a coastal species, it is also one of the most difficult to observe. Porpoises show little of their backs during normal surfacing, and any swell or wave action may shield them from view. Even in perfect sighting conditions, an observer must have keen eyes to identify a surfacing harbour porpoise.

Of course, groups are much easier to spot than individuals; most groups contain two to five individuals. Although rare, aggregations of hundreds of porpoises have been observed. These are likely feeding rather than social groups.

1 METRE

In general, harbour porpoise are most commonly seen alone and are considered relatively nonsocial.

Harbour porpoise are found only in the northern hemisphere, in temperate to subarctic waters. Although they are most common in continental shelf waters, and even enter shallow bays, estuaries, and tidal channels, they can be found in deeper offshore waters. Individual harbour porpoises are highly mobile and may inhabit home ranges of thousands of square kilometres. Although the global geographic range of harbour porpoise is large, its distribution is not continuous. As a result, in the North Atlantic alone 14 subpopulations have been suggested.

Distinguishing characteristics

Harbour porpoises are robust, chunky cetaceans characterized by their small size, lack of a prominent beak, and a dark triangular dorsal fin with a broad base and blunt tip. Similar to most cetaceans, they exhibit countershading—a black or dark grey back and a white throat and belly. Their sides display a mix of these two shades, often interpreted as light grey with black flecks merging the two opposite pigments. Colouration is asymmetrical on both sides. Most harbour porpoises have a dark chin and dark pectoral fins and flukes on both surfaces.

The dorsal fin is located approximately mid-length along the back and is the most noticeable feature when the porpoise surfaces. Surfacing harbour porpoises appear as a slow forward-rolling triangular fin with otherwise little noticeable body above the water. They travel at slow speeds, although they have been observed swimming fast and erratically. It is unusual to see aerial action from harbour porpoises except when they leap above the water's surface (porpoising) in chase of prey. Unlike other dolphins and porpoises, harbour porpoise do not normally bow- or wake-ride but avoid boats.

During calm ocean conditions and under the right light conditions, the harbour porpoise's blow can sometimes be seen. Their breathing can be heard under the right conditions as a puffing or sneezing sound. Because of this, fishers in Atlantic Canada and New England often call them "puffing pigs," "puffers," "squealers," or "screamers."

Feeding and behaviour

On the population level, harbour porpoises take a variety of prey, including fish and cephalopods such as squid and octopus. Harbour porpoise feed alone. Schooling fish such as herring and capelin make up the majority of their diet, although this varies by region and availability. Because of their feeding preferences, harbour porpoises are named "herring hogs" by Maine fishers.

Harbour porpoise have a relatively short lifespan but can be highly fertile. Females reach sexual maturity between three and four years of age, early on the cetacean scale. Harbour porpoise can be pregnant for several consecutive years, necessitating an overlap of lactation and a subsequent pregnancy, which results in considerable nutritional stress.

Harbour porpoise produce acoustic sounds ranging from about 40 Hz to 160 kHz, an extraordinary range for a cetacean. High-frequency echolocation clicks are narrow-band signals used for both object discrimination and bearing detection. Their low-frequency repertoire is less studied but may be important for communication and other social functions.

Population status

Harbour porpoise are widespread and abundant in their global geographic range and are listed as Least Concern by the IUCN. Over 14 subpopulations have been described and, in at least two regions where there is a harbour porpoise hunt, population declines have been observed.

Although the range of the harbour porpoise's habitat has not been surveyed,

Harbour porpoise are often difficult to spot, due to their small size; the triangular dorsal fin is often the only feature visible to observers. *Nadine and Thierry Vogenstahl*

A harbour porpoise photographed in the Baltic Sea, near Denmark. *Florian Graner / SeaPics.com*

a minimum global population of 700,000 is estimated. While the global population trend of harbour porpoises is unknown, evidence of population declines in some regions exists, including the Baltic Sea, Black Sea, and inland waterways of Washington state.

Threats

The most significant threats to harbour porpoise are deliberate and incidental takes. They were hunted in the Bay of Fundy, Gulf of St. Lawrence, and Newfoundland and Labrador in Atlantic Canada. Although most fisheries for harbour porpoises are closed, Greenland continues to take harbour porpoises annually. Hunts in some regions, such as the Black Sea, have killed hundreds of thousands within the last five decades. The effects of these hunts are still felt, although the ultimate impact remains undocumented.

Incidental catches in fishing gear, particularly gill-nets, is the greatest threat to the harbour porpoise. Documentation from the United States, Atlantic Canada, West Greenland, North Sea, British Isles, and other areas show many thousands are being caught annually in fishing gear.

Harbour porpoise are at risk from threats common to most marine mammals, including chemical and contaminant exposure, vessel and boat traffic, underwater noise, and prey depletion from overfishing and invasive and competitive species. Only a few regions, such as American, Canadian, and European shelf waters, have implemented conservation actions, while in many more regions subpopulations may be at risk and unprotected.

GLOSSARY

Aggregation: A large gathering of individuals or groups.

Anthropogenic: Human-made; anthropogenic sound is human-made underwater sound pollution.

Baleen: Plates composed of keratin hanging from a mysticete's upper jaw along the outer perimeter on each side of its mouth. The baleen's inner surface is composed of fringe, which filters out water during feeding, keeping prey inside the whale's mouth.

Benthopelagic: Referring to organisms that can live and feed on or near the bottom (*benthos*), in midwater (*pelagic*), and at the surface.

Blowhole: Hole on the top of a cetacean's head through which it breathes; odontocetes have a single hole, mysticetes' are segmented into two.

Bow-ride: When cetaceans, especially dolphins, ride on the bow waves produced by a boat or vessel as its bow cuts through the water's surface.

Breach: When a whale leaps fully or partially out of the water.

Callosities: Raised patches of skin tissue, like a callus, typically on the heads and jaws of right and bowhead whales; used for identification of individuals.

Cephalopod: A type of marine mollusk, including (but not limited to) squid, octopuses, and cuttlefish.

Coda: Acoustic signals produced by sperm whales for socializing, consisting of patterns of clicks shared among individuals and which contain a repertoire of multiple patterns.

Continental slope, continental slope edge: Slope linking the continental shelf to the deep ocean bottom; edge refers to approximately where the slope descent begins.

Copepods: Group of over 1,000 species of small crustaceans, some of which are important prey for some cetaceans, and range from microscopic to 1 centimetre in length.

Delphinidae: Scientific family composed of all oceanic dolphins.

Dimorphic: Exhibiting difference in morphology, especially sexual dimorphism, in which there is a difference in morphology between males and females of the same species.

Dorsal fin: Fin on the back, or dorsal surface, of organisms.

Echelon: Side-by-side orientation of a pair of individuals, mother-offspring, and group members, especially exhibited by sperm whales and dolphins.

Echolocation: Form of communication in which a sound pulse is emitted from an animal, bounces off an object, and returns to the animal, thus allowing it to discriminate between objects. All odontocetes echolocate; often for feeding purposes.

Euphausiid: Small shrimp-like crustaceans, including krill; important prey for some cetaceans.

Extralimital: Not found within the organism's natural population or species geographic range.

Falcate: Sickle-shaped, or exhibiting extreme curve; often refers to dorsal fin shape.

Flipper slap: When a whale or dolphin slaps its pectoral fins, or flippers, on the water's surface.

Fluke up: When a whale or dolphin raises its tail fin, or fluke, above the water's surface as it begins a terminal dive.

Fluke: Tail fin of cetaceans.

Generation time: The time interval between an individual's birth and its first offspring.

Great Whales: The 13 largest whale species in the world; 12 mysticetes and one odontocete: bowhead, North Atlantic right, North pacific right, southern right, gray, blue, fin, sei, Bryde's, common minke, Antarctic minke, humpback, and sperm whales.

Group size: Number of individuals within a particular group of animals, generally of the same species.

Gulf Stream: Large warm surface current originating in the Gulf of Mexico, travelling northward off the United States' east coast, skirting the shelf edge offshore, eventually leading to the British Isles and Scandinavia.

Habitat: The natural and physical environment in which a particular species lives.

International Union for Conservation of Nature (IUCN): An international body for the conservation and preservation of natural habitats, environments, and species.

International Whaling Commission (IWC): International intergovernmental organization for the conservation and protection of whales, including the management of all forms of whaling.

Labrador Current: The cold, southward-flowing surface current originating in the Canadian Arctic north of Labrador, travelling down the Labrador shelf, around Newfoundland, and southwestward along the Scotian Shelf.

Lobtailing: When a cetacean is positioned vertically in the water column with its head down and its tail and a portion of its tail stock above the water's surface, often appearing to wave its tail or slap it at the surface. See *Tail slap*.

Lunge feeding: Behaviour exhibited by many cetaceans, especially mysticetes. A whale accelerates to the surface with its mouth open to engulf prey, usually partially erupting through the water's surface.

Melon: Oval-shaped fatty organ in the forehead of all odontocetes, believed to be used for sound production and reception.

Mesoplodont: Fourteen species in the genus *Mesoplodon*, all of which are deep-diving beaked whales.

Migration: Mass movement of animals, typically over great distances, for purposes such as feeding and breeding in two geographically and ecologically distinct areas. Humpback and gray whale migrations are among the best understood.

Modern whaling period: Beginning in approximately the late 1800s, technological advances enabled whalers to more effectively kill, capture, and process specimens. Cannon-fired harpoons and steam-powered boats allowed for the quick decimation of many whale populations worldwide.

Morbillivirus: Virus that causes disease in some species of animals and humans, including marine animals. Transmission between infected marine mammals and humans is a possibility if contact with an animal occurs.

Mysids: Small, chiefly marine, shrimp-like crustaceans.

Mysticete: Baleen whales within the suborder Mysticeti.

Ocean noise: Any noise or acoustic disturbance in the ocean, ranging from natural sources (rain, wind, earthquakes, biological sources, etc.) to anthropogenic sounds (vessel traffic, fishing noise, seismic activities, naval sonar, etc.).

Odontocete: Cetaceans within the suborder Odontoceti. These are all toothed whales and dolphins; the function of the teeth is not limited to feeding.

Pack ice: Large sheets of ice, driven together by wind or currents to form a single mass of ice.

Pectoral fin: The fins on the forward lateral sides of the animals; also referred to as flippers.

Population (biology): All individuals of a species or subgroup of species geographically and biologically capable of interbreeding.

Porpoising: A type of swimming behaviour; the whale or dolphin swims quickly near the surface of the water, breaking the surface at frequent intervals.

Productivity, biological productivity: Production of organic or biological matter. High productivity rates are often associated with high plant growth (phytoplankton), leading to higher secondary growth of microscopic and macroscopic animals.

Range: The geographic boundaries of an animal's movement or habitat area.

Reproductively active: Capable of reproducing.

Rorqual: Of the family Balaenopteridae; this division of mysticete is characterized by its streamlined form, dorsal fin, and ventral pleats.

Rostrum: The cetacean's upper jaw or snout.

Saddle patch: The light white to grey patch behind the dorsal fin, present on killer whales and pilot whales, among others.

Skim feeders, skim-feeding: Feeding behaviour of a cetacean, typically a mysticete; it swims at the water's surface with its mouth open, engulfing water and filtering out prey through its baleen.

Species (biology): Group of populations (see *Population [biology]*) capable of interbreeding and sexually isolated from other species. Can be divided into subspecies.

Splashguard: The raised tissue in front of a cetacean's blowhole, especially mysticetes, to prevent water from entering the blowhole as the whale surfaces to breathe.

Spyhop: When a whale or dolphin, oriented vertically in the water column, surfaces with its head above the water's surface.

Stock (biology): Subpopulation of a species in which characteristics such as growth, recruitment, and mortality are used to determine population dynamics. Often used in government assessments of subpopulations within certain geographic and political boundaries.

Stranding: When a marine animal swims onto shore, becoming stuck. Also referred to as beaching.

Tail slap: Surface whale behaviour; it remains submerged except for its tail, which it slaps back and forth on the water's surface.

Tail stock: The narrow, muscular portion of the animal's body preceding the fluke. Also referred to as a caudal peduncle.

Taxonomy: Classification and identification of biological organisms into a hierarchical system based on natural and genetic relationships.

Terminal dive: Dive at the end of the cetacean's surfacing sequence in which the animal proceeds to depth. Also referred to as a sounding dive.

The Gully: An area on the Scotian Shelf, off Nova Scotia, characterized by a large, deep underwater canyon inhabited by many cetaceans, particularly beaked whale species.

Thermocline: Region or layer in the vertical water column in which temperature rapidly changes from the warmer surface water, also known as the mixed layer, to the colder deep water.

Thoracic patch: Yellowish patch on both sides of the common dolphin's forward flank.

Tonal call, pulsed tonal call: Vocalizations of a narrow frequency band.

Trophic level: Position, or energy level, of an organism within a food chain.

Unerupted: Teeth that have not come up above the skin's surface on the jaw.

Ventral: Bottom surface; underside.

Vestigial (biology): Remaining anatomical structures, such as vestigial teeth, that no longer serve a purpose.

Vocalizations: Sounds produced for communication; also called "calls."

Wake-ride: When cetaceans, especially dolphins, ride on wake waves produced by a boat or vessel as it moves.

Ziphiidae: Taxonomic family which includes all beaked whales; characterized by relatively elongated beaks and deep diving capabilities.

FURTHER READING

Bortolotti, Dan. *Wild Blue: A Natural History of the World's Largest Animal.* New York: St. Martin's Press, 2008.

Dickinson, Anthony and Chesley W. Sanger. *Twentieth-Century Shore-Station Whaling in Newfoundland and Labrador.* Montreal: McGill-Queen's University Press, 2005.

Ford, John K.B. and Graeme M. Ellis. *Transients: Mammal-Hunting Killer Whales of British Columbia, Washington, and Southeastern Alaska.* Vancouver: University of British Columbia Press, 1999.

Ford, John K.B., Graeme M. Ellis, and Kenneth C. Balcomb. *Killer Whales: The Natural History and Genealogy of* Orcinus Orca *in British Columbia and Washington State.* Seattle: University of Washington Press, 2000.

Mann, Janet, Richard C. Connor, Peter L. Tyack, and Hal Whitehead, eds. *Cetacean Societies: Field Studies of Dolphins and Whales.* Chicago: University of Chicago Press, 2000.

Parsons, Edward C.M. *An Introduction to Marine Mammal Biology and Conservation.* Burlington, MA: Jones & Bartlett Learning, LLC, 2013.

Perrin, W.F., Bernd Wursig, and J.G.M. Thewissen, eds. *Encyclopedia of Marine Mammals.* 2nd ed. Burlington, MA: Academic Press, 2008.

Reeves, Randall R., B.S. Stewart, P.J. Clapham, and J.A. Powell. *National Audubon Society Guide to Marine Mammals of the World.* New York: Chanticleer Press, Inc., 2002.

Vogenstahl, Nadine and Thierry Vogenstahl. *Saint-Pierre-et-Miquelon Balades en Mer «Whalecome».* France: Écrevolles à Troyes, 2009.

Whitehead, Hal. *Sperm Whales: Social Evolution in the Ocean.* Chicago: University of Chicago Press, 2003.

ACKNOWLEDGEMENTS

This book represents work and collaboration from colleagues and friends over many years and would not have been possible without their help, knowledge, and guidance. In that respect, I want especially to thank Jack Lawson, Sean Todd, and John Anderson—my graduate and undergraduate supervisors, mentors, colleagues, and friends. I want to acknowledge all of the people who have helped me by accepting me into their labs and working directly with me, especially John Ford, Hal Whitehead, David Mellinger, Wayne Ledwell, and colleagues too many to list.

The preparation of this book was aided by the many individuals who contributed personal and professional photographs. I am indebted to Nadine and Thierry Vogenstahl for perhaps the most amazing photographs of whales and dolphins in the northwest Atlantic. I also thank DFO, John G.T. Anderson, Marie Auger-Méthé, Joana Augusto, Robin Baird, Robert Basha, Marina Milligan, Kristin O'Brien, Pierre Richard, and the Whitehead Lab of Dalhousie University for contributing photographs.

I wish to thank my editor, Stephanie Porter, for maintaining faith in this book and her hard work to keep the book on track.

Finally, I wouldn't be where I am today without the support and belief from my parents. My mother, Trish Stevens, illustrated this book; it is an honour to produce a book with such an amazing artist. Thanks are in order for Robby Basha for keeping me going during the writing of this book. And, of course, my beloved pups, Hailey and Rocky, deserve credit for being at my side, every step of the way.

For everybody who has helped me along the way and directly with the content of this book, I thank you. I could not have done this without you.

Photo by Robert Basha

ABOUT THE AUTHOR

Tara S. Stevens is a PhD candidate at the Graduate School of Oceanography at the University of Rhode Island in Narragansett, Rhode Island. Her dissertation is on the behaviour and ecology of killer whales in the northwest Atlantic. Tara attended New York University in New York City and received her Bachelor's degree from College of the Atlantic in Bar Harbor, Maine. She now resides in North Kingstown, Rhode Island, with her partner, Robert Basha, and their six dogs and two cats.

Stevens has spent nearly 10 years studying the whales and dolphins of the northwest Atlantic, mostly with the Department of Fisheries and Oceans (DFO) based in St. John's, Newfoundland and Labrador. Her research projects have taken her from Labrador to the West Indies. She has also worked with Pacific killer whale populations with DFO in Nanaimo, British Columbia. Her research interests include the social and feeding behaviour of cetaceans, particularly killer whales, underwater sound analyses, and how killer whale populations in the northwest Atlantic compare to others worldwide.

ABOUT THE ILLUSTRATOR

An artist and illustrator for over 30 years, Trish Stevens works with a variety of media, including watercolour, acrylic, oil, and pen and ink, and she creates extraordinarily life-like depictions of animals and landscapes. She lives in Maine. This book is the first collaboration between Stevens and her daughter, Tara S. Stevens.

Photo by Jeremiah Stevens